British Colonialism and the Criminalization of Homosexuality

British Colonialism and the Criminalization of Homosexuality examines whether colonial rule is responsible for the historical, and continuing, criminalization of same-sex sexual relations in many parts of the world.

Enze Han and Joseph O'Mahoney gather and assess historical evidence to demonstrate the different ways in which the British empire spread laws criminalizing homosexual conduct amongst its colonies. Evidence includes case studies of former British colonies and the common law and criminal codes like the Indian Penal Code of 1860 and the Queensland Criminal Code of 1899. Surveying a wide range of countries, the authors scrutinize whether ex-British colonies are more likely to have laws that criminalize homosexual conduct than other ex-colonies or other states in general. They interrogate the claim that British imperialism uniquely 'poisoned' societies against homosexuality, and look at the legacies of colonialism and the politics and legal status of homosexuality across the globe.

Enze Han is Associate Professor at the Department of Politics and Public Administration at the University of Hong Kong. He has a PhD from George Washington University, USA, and is a member of the School of Social Science at the Institute for Advanced Study in Princeton, USA. He used to teach at SOAS, University of London, UK.

Joseph O'Mahoney is Lecturer in Politics and International Relations at the University of Reading and a Research Fellow in the Security Studies Program at the Massachusetts Institute of Technology, USA. He has a PhD from George Washington University, USA, and has held positions at Brown University, Seton Hall University, and Regis College.

British Colonialism and the Criminalization of Homosexuality

Queens, Crime and Empire

Enze Han and Joseph O'Mahoney

Routledge
Taylor & Francis Group
LONDON AND NEW YORK

First published 2018
by Routledge
2 Park Square, Milton Park, Abingdon, Oxon OX14 4RN

and by Routledge
711 Third Avenue, New York, NY 10017

Routledge is an imprint of the Taylor & Francis Group, an informa business

British Library Cataloguing-in-Publication Data
A catalogue record for this book is available from the British Library

Library of Congress Cataloging-in-Publication Data
Names: Han, Enze, author. | O'Mahoney, Joseph P. A., author.
Title: British colonialism and the criminalization of homosexuality : queens, crime and empire / Enze Han and Joseph O'Mahoney.
Description: London ; New York : Routledge, 2018. | Includes bibliographical references and index.
Identifiers: LCCN 2018006793 | ISBN 9780815367925 (hardback : alk. paper) | ISBN 9781351256209 (ebook)
Subjects: LCSH: Homosexuality—Great Britain—Colonies—History. | Homosexuality—Law and legislation—Great Britain—Colonies—History. | Sex crimes—Great Britain—Colonies—History. | Gay rights—Great Britain—Colonies—History. | Great Britain—Colonies—Administration—History.
Classification: LCC HQ76.3.G7 H36 2018 | DDC 306.76/60941—dc23
LC record available at https://lccn.loc.gov/2018006793

ISBN: 978-0-8153-6792-5 (hbk)
ISBN: 978-1-351-25620-9 (ebk)

Typeset in Times New Roman
by Apex CoVantage, LLC

Contents

Acknowledgments

This book came about through a rather random occasion. In 2014, we published an article "British Colonialism and the Criminalization of Homosexuality" in the *Cambridge Review of International Affairs*. Since the publication of that article, we have constantly received interest from the public about the legacy of British colonialism on LGBT issues. Then, in May 2017, we received an email from Alexandra McGregor, who is the editor for Gender and Sexuality Studies at Routledge and who wanted us to develop our article into a book for the Routledge Focus series. Without her support and the encouragement from two reviewers we would not have had the determination to put together this book. We also want to thank Kitty Imbert at Routledge for her help throughout the writing process. Our thanks also go to Taylor and Francis and the *Cambridge Review of International Affairs* for permission to reuse some material from our article.

Joseph would like to thank MIT libraries for tirelessly sourcing materials; Regis College especially for having a long winter break; and, as always, Nancy, Addy, and Cam for all of their various types of support. Enze would like to thank SOAS, University of London, for the library access, and the Leverhulme Trust for the teaching buyout during the 2017 academic year. Enze also would like to thank Iris Lim for her excellent research assistance. Finally, this book was written during the transition period when Enze moved from SOAS to the University of Hong Kong, so he would like to thank the people at HKU for making his transition easier. All remaining errors are of course our own.

1 Introduction

In January 2018, the Indian Supreme Court ordered a review of section 377 of the Indian penal code (IPC).[1] This section criminalizes consensual sex between men, with a possible sentence of life imprisonment. Why does India have such a law? Does its origin lie in ancient religious or cultural taboos on homosexuality? Did the recent rise in Hindu nationalism lead to a crackdown on perceived deviance? Was there an upsurge in Indian civil society against Lesbian, Gay, Bisexual, and Transgender (LGBT) lifestyles? No. In fact, this law was imposed during the British Raj over 150 years ago and has remained unchanged since. Was India singularly unlucky in this regard, a victim of the oddities of historical happenstance? If we look at Singapore, or Malaysia, or Brunei, each country has a law, numbered section 377, or 377A, criminalizing homosexual conduct to some degree. This is not a coincidence. These laws were also imposed during British imperial rule and have survived to the present. In this book, we show that, in fact, many other countries have laws proscribing sexual relations between men that date back in some way to the influence of the British Empire.[2]

At a time when many in the West have already been celebrating the legalization of same-sex marriage, it is still a daunting reality that homosexuality remains a punishable crime in countries around the world. The most recent report released by the International Lesbian, Gay, Bisexual, Trans and Intersex Association (ILGA) shows that, although consensual homosexual conduct is legal in 124 states and territories, there are still 72 countries that continue the criminalization of homosexual relations.[3] In many of these places, LGBT communities continue to face persecution because of their sexual orientation and many face lengthy imprisonment and cruel treatment. For example, in May 2010, a gay couple in Malawi was found guilty of "unnatural acts" and faced charges of up to 14 years in prison, under sections 153 and 156 of Malawi's criminal code.[4] Similarly, in 2014, two Ugandan men were also tried on the charge of homosexuality and faced possible life imprisonment.[5] Worse still is that in some countries, homosexual conduct can even lead to the death penalty. In September 2011, three men were executed for sodomy in Iran.[6] These executions were all undertaken with reference to articles 108 and 110 of the Islamic penal code.

While these scenes are horrific, there is cause for hope. In a wide variety of countries, social attitudes towards the LGBT community are becoming ever more tolerant, and efforts to decriminalize homosexuality have been ongoing. The Indian case has been a roller coaster in recent years. On July 3, 2009, New Delhi's High Court ruled that homosexual conduct should not be deemed a criminal offense, challenging more than a century of criminalization of homosexuality in India since the British introduced the IPC in 1862. However, four years later, in 2013, after appeals made by religious groups, the Indian Supreme Court reversed that ruling saying that it was up to parliament to legislate on the issue. At the time of writing this legal battle in India is still ongoing.[7] More hopefully, several countries have successfully decriminalized consensual homosexual conduct. The Turkish Republic of Northern Cyprus, a non-state entity unrecognized except by Turkey, reformed its penal code in 2014, removing such criminalization, making it the last territory in Europe to have decriminalized homosexuality. Elsewhere, several sovereign states have got rid of their sodomy laws in the last few years. For example, Nauru in the South Pacific[8] and Seychelles in the Indian Ocean[9] legalized homosexuality in May 2016. Later that year, Belize's Supreme Court overturned its law criminalizing homosexual conduct.[10] So considerable progress has recently been made to remove the legal restrictions of the past.

These last three countries are all former British colonial possessions of one type or another. The link between British colonialism and currently having anti-gay laws is strong. Of the 72 countries with such a law in 2018, at least 38 of them were once subject to some sort of British colonial rule.[11] This kind of correlation seems convincing on its face, but is there any additional reason to think that these laws are actually the result of, or the fault of, the British Empire?

The legacies of British colonialism

There has been a rich literature detailing the impact of colonialism on the rest of the world. For some, western colonialism is at the very root of underdevelopment in the developing world, because colonial powers not only plundered natural resources of the colonies, but "colonialism created ineffective legal-administrative institutions, empowered local chiefs and notables, and thereby institutionalized decentralized and despotic systems of control."[12] Furthermore, western colonialism has been blamed for the impoverishment, violence, and destruction of indigenous forms of knowledge, culture, and property. However, for many others, the legacies of western colonialism are much more nuanced. Instead, many studies have found that the identity of the colonizer matters a great deal for the socioeconomic and cultural institutions of postcolonial countries, which in turn affects the economic growth rates of these countries.[13] Others have also found that different colonial experiences are closely associated with countries' democratic credentials and survival.[14]

Some have argued that there have been positive contributions brought by British colonialism to some of their former colonies.[15] Lange, Mahoney, and vom Hau, for example, argue that the colonialism of liberal Britain, in comparison with mercantilist Spain, tended to produce positive effects in its colonies' economic development. That is, British colonialism spread a liberal model that "organizes productive activity toward maximizing profit through exchange in free markets . . . [and] political authorities use the state to uphold private property, encourage commercial production, and enforce the rule of law."[16] The common law legal system introduced or imposed by the British has also been lauded for its better protection of property rights and contribution to better government performance as well as being a better guarantee for freedom.[17] Furthermore, British colonialism has been credited for its positive legacy on democratic development in its former colonies.[18] The parliamentary system, election for local self-governing bodies, superior infrastructure, and indirect ruling style have all been pointed out as indicators of the benign British colonial legacy and causes for healthier democratic development in former British colonies.[19] Other studies have found much more mixed results, such as Verghese's finding that provinces of India formerly ruled by the British experience more caste and tribal violence in contemporary India, but former princely states experience more religious conflict.[20]

As we show in this book, one particularly dark legacy left by British colonial history is that British colonialism might have been especially detrimental towards LGBT rights in colonial societies. From 1860 onwards, the British Empire spread a specific set of legal codes and common law throughout its colonies including the prominent examples of the colonial criminal codes of India and Queensland, both of which specifically criminalized male-to-male sexual relations, though by long-term imprisonment rather than death. For example, section 377 of the Indian penal code (IPC) read as follows:

> Section 377: Unnatural offences – Whoever voluntarily has carnal intercourse against the order of nature with any man, woman or animal shall be punished with imprisonment for life, or with imprisonment . . . for a term which may extend to 10 years, and shall be liable to fine.
>
> Explanation – Penetration is sufficient to constitute the carnal intercourse necessary to the offense described in this Section.

The IPC was the first comprehensive codified criminal law produced anywhere in the British Empire.[21] Fearful that its "soldiers and colonial administrators – particularly those without wives at hand – would turn to sodomy in these decadent, hot surroundings," the British Empire drafted the IPC with the intention of both protecting the Christians from "corruption" as well as correcting and Christianizing "native" custom.[22] At the time, British colonial judicial officers were often inexperienced lay magistrates without legal resources and relied upon importing extant examples of criminal regulations. Thus, the IPC, together with the Queensland criminal code of 1899 (QCC), and others, became the model for many British colonies' legal systems, and was exported and imposed on various other British colonial acquisitions throughout Asia, Africa, and beyond. Thus, through its colonial administration, the British managed to impose and institutionalize a set of laws in its colonies that criminalized homosexual conduct.

In contrast with the British experience, the other big colonial power – France – left a very different institutional legacy as regards consensual homosexual conduct. Due to developments in Enlightenment concepts of liberty and rights after the French Revolution, the French penal code of 1791 decriminalized sodomy between overage consenting adults in private. This code was subsequently spread by Napoleon's conquests in continental Europe and through the French Empire.[23] The French thus did not leave the same institutional legacy on its colonies that the British did. These historical institutional legacies may have had more of an influence on current national laws than other factors that are more specific to LGBT rights in particular. Sanders takes a strongly stated position on the role of colonialism: "Of the great colonial powers of Western Europe – Britain, France, Germany, the Netherlands, Portugal and Spain – only Britain left this legacy to its colonies."[24] The claim that countries once colonized by the British are more likely to have such criminalization legislation in their law books is prominent in the literature. However, such a claim has so far not been adequately evaluated.

Argument and structure of the book

This book represents an effort to document the legacy of British colonialism on the criminalization of homosexuality throughout the world. In this book, we not only look at how British colonial administrations introduced a variety of legal codes that included provisions targeted at homosexual conduct, but we also analyze the longevity of such a legal legacy. Specifically, has it been more difficult for post-independence countries with a British legacy to get rid of criminalization?

First, we look at the historical evidence of whether and how colonies received their criminalization laws from the British Empire. As is common in imperial history, there are multifarious situations and processes. We find some clear-cut cases of direct imposition, some cases of informal influence of various types, and we also discover that in some cases the current laws cannot, in fact, be attributed to the British legacy. The second type of evidence that we investigate is a large-n dataset of 185 countries. We use systematic data analysis to find out whether modern states are more likely to currently criminalize homosexuality if they were a British colony than if they were not. We also ask whether former British colonies are less likely or slower to decriminalize on average than the former colonies of other European imperialists. In order to deal with several plausible alternative hypotheses, we control for numerous other variables that might be expected to influence the likelihood of repressive LGBT rights legislation, like religion, wealth, democracy, and others.

The book also includes two chapters that discuss in detail several former British colonies and their histories of continual criminalization of homosexuality versus another set of such former colonies who have successfully gotten rid of such laws. For the ones that continue to criminalize homosexuality, we provide a detailed analysis of the historical origins of such laws in these countries and of the political processes that have prevented these countries from removing them. Although the enforcement of such laws varies, from Uganda's active persecution of LGBT persons to Singapore's rare instances of penalization, it remains true that such laws have prolonged the stigmatization of the LGBT community. Through such analyses, we also examine different political logics that are in play that have prolonged the criminalization of homosexuality. On the other hand, there are a handful of countries that have made significant progress toward greater social inclusion of their sexual minorities in the recent past. In this book we document the political and legal processes that have caused such changes, and we explore the political and social consequences for the LGBT community.

The structure of the book is as follows. In Chapter 2, we investigate the historical processes of the spread of laws criminalizing homosexual conduct in the British Empire. Then, in Chapter 3, we present systematic empirical analysis of data on 185 countries. Chapter 4 examines six former British colonies – India, Singapore, Guyana, Jamaica, Uganda, and Kenya – and the prolonged agony of the LGBT communities in these countries under the legal prohibition of homosexuality. Chapter 5 analyzes another six former British colonies – Hong Kong, South Africa, Belize, Fiji, Cyprus, and Seychelles – for the dynamics of decriminalization across different political contexts. Chapter 6 concludes with some reflections of the causal mechanisms of legal changes on the issue of criminalization of homosexuality, as well as a projection of the future trajectories of LGBT rights globally.

Pre-colonial sexuality

Since our book's primary concern is how British colonialism has brought the penalization of homosexuality to its colonies, it is necessary to pay some special attention to the issue of sexuality before the arrival of colonialism. In discussing pre-colonial sexuality, it is crucial to keep in mind that we want to avoid the fallacy of methodological nationalism,[25] in that many of the countries today did not have clear territorial boundaries set during the pre-colonial period, and in fact many of them were the product of colonization. Thus, when we discuss the relationship between colonization and homosexuality before the start of British colonialization, we are really commenting on these histories on the basis of regionally or culturally based customs, broadly speaking, as opposed to national borders as they currently exist. At the same time, when we discuss pre-colonial homosexual practices, it is also very difficult to pinpoint when colonialism started to introduce homophobia or how colonial experiences began to influence local sexual practices. Such clear binary boundaries might be very difficult to clearly define. Likewise, we also need to reject a binary conceptualization of whether pre-colonial societies accepted or rejected homosexual behavior before and/or after colonization because it is very difficult to define exactly what was or wasn't homosexuality in pre-colonial societies. This is so because in parts of the world where these categories were not yet widely known, for people who performed homosexual acts their sexual orientations were not necessarily their identifications.[26] We need to keep in mind that homosexual conduct was often muddled with different ways sexual behaviors manifested across different cultural contexts.[27]

Having said that, we want to point out that much of the literature on sexuality would confirm that homosexual conduct was widely prevalent throughout the world before the arrival of European colonialism. As Murray and Roscoe pointed out, in pre-colonial Africa, for example, three basic patterns of homosexual relationships – egalitarian, age-stratified, and gender-based – were all represented.[28] Many of these relationships were often institutionalized, and were not uncommon for both males and females before marriage.[29] This is also the case in Latin America, where the Spanish were "shocked" by the homosexual behavior that they witnessed. And indeed, the Spanish used the justifications of such "negative" portrayal of the "morally degraded" practices to justify their rule and the exploitation of the native Americans in the New World.[30] Homosexuality was also prevalent historically in Asia. For instance, in pre-modern China, homoerotic relationships between men were often treated as an intellectual refinement seeking "the satisfaction of both the senses and the spirit," and the public was general indifferent to them.[31] In vernacular stories, homosexual conduct among men was often humorously and positively depicted, rather than morally condemned.[32] Similarly, in pre-colonial India, Ruth Vanita comments that "same-sex love and romantic friendships existed without any extended history of overt persecution."[33] Indeed, it was the British colonial administrators who imported the overall homophobic attitudes into India, which led to the fact that "a minority puritanical and homophobic voice in India became mainstream."[34]

European colonialism also has had a clear impact on how local communities perceive homosexuality. In the African context, although there was little indigenous writing on the subject, almost all the early documentation of homosexuality in Africa was written by these European colonial actors, who overwhelmingly used moral rhetoric to describe homosexual acts as "unnatural" or "sinful." These moral discourses, "in which sexual identities, roles, and acts were represented in the terms of a Judeo-Christian code," have made a fundamental imprint on later discourses on African homosexuality.[35] Thus, although some of the homophobic rhetoric from Africa, or indeed elsewhere in the world, tends to portray homosexuality as corruption imported by the morally debauched West, they nonetheless continued the same moral versus immoral trope inherited from the colonial past.[36]

Be that as it may, despite some of these contemporary controversies regarding pre-colonial sexuality in the global context, this book aims to demonstrate how British colonialism has played a crucial role in spreading a particular set of legal codes around the world and the overwhelming consequences in criminalizing homosexuality. The next chapter details this historical development.

Notes

1 Michael Safi, "India's Highest Court to Review Colonial-Era Law Criminalising Gay Sex," *The Guardian*, January 8, 2018.
2 Enze Han and Joseph O'Mahoney, "British Colonialism and the Criminalization of Homosexuality," *Cambridge Review of International Affairs* 27, no. 2 (2014): 268–88.
3 Aengus Carroll and Lucas Ramon Mendos, "State-Sponsored Homophobia: A World Survey of Sexual Orientation Laws," *ILGA* (2017), 8.
4 Barry Bearak, "Gay Couple Convicted in Malawi," *New York Times*, May 18, 2010.
5 Barbara Among, "Ugandan Men to Go on Trial on Homosexuality Charges," *The Guardian*, April 17, 2014.
6 Saeed Kamali Dehghan, "Iran Executes Three Men on Homosexuality Charges," *The Guardian*, September 7, 2011.

7 Safi, "India's Highest Court to Review Colonial-Era Law Criminalising Gay Sex."

8 Ben Doherty, "Nauru Decriminalises Homosexuality and Suicide," *The Guardian*, May 29, 2016.

9 Dan Avery, "Seychelles Votes to Decriminalize Homosexuality," *New Now Next*, May 18, 2016.

10 Brooke Sopelsa, "Belize Supreme Court Overturns Anti-Gay Law," *NBC News*, August 10, 2016.

11 We discuss different types of British colonial rule in Chapters 2 and 3.

12 Matthew Lange, *Lineages of Despotism and Development: British Colonialism and State Power* (Chicago: University of Chicago Press, 2009), 9.

13 David S. Landes, *The Wealth and Poverty of Nations: Why Some Are So Rich and Some So Poor* (New York: W. W. Norton, 1999); William F. S. Miles, *Hausaland Divided: Colonialism and Independence in Nigeria and Niger* (Ithaca, NY: Cornell University Press, 1994); Crawford Young, *The African Colonial State in Comparative Perspective* (New Haven, CT: Yale University Press, 1997); M. S. Alam, "Colonialism, Decolonisation and Growth Rates: Theory and Empirical Evidence," *Cambridge Journal of Economics* 18, no. 3 (June 1, 1994): 235–58.

14 Michael Bernhard, Christopher Reenock, and Timothy Nordstrom, "The Legacy of Western Overseas Colonialism on Democratic Survival," *International Studies Quarterly* 48, no. 1 (2004): 225–50; Ola Olsson, "On the Democratic Legacy of Colonialism," *Journal of Comparative Economics* 37, no. 4 (2009): 534–51.

15 Niall Ferguson, *Empire: The Rise and Demise of the British World Order and the Lessons for Global Power* (New York: Basic Books, 2003).

16 Matthew Lange, James Mahoney, and Matthias vom Hau, "Colonialism and Development: A Comparative Analysis of Spanish and British Colonies," *American Journal of Sociology* 111, no. 5 (2006): 1416.

17 Rafael LaPorta, Florencio Lopez-de-Silanes, Andrei Shleifer, and Robert Vishny, "The Quality of Government," *Journal of Law, Economics and Organization* 15, no. 1 (1999): 222–79; Rafael La Porta, Florencio López-de-Silanes, Cristian Pop-Eleches, and Andrei Shleifer, "Judicial Checks and Balances," *Journal of Political Economy* 112, no. 2 (2004): 445–70.

18 Samuel P. Huntington, "Will More Countries Become Democratic?," *Political Science Quarterly* 99, no. 2 (1984): 193–218; Seymour Martin Lipset, *A Comparative Analysis of the Social Requisites of Democracy* (Oxford: Blackwell Publishers, 2004).

19 Bernhard, Reenock and Nordstrom, "The Legacy of Western Overseas Colonialism on Democratic Survival."

20 Ajay Verghese, *The Colonial Origins of Ethnic Violence in India* (Stanford, CA: Stanford University Press, 2016).

21 Martin L. Friedland, "Codification in the Commonwealth: Earlier Efforts," *Commonwealth Law Bulletin* 18, no. 3 (1992): 1172.

22 Alok Gupta, *This Alien Legacy: The Origins of "Sodomy" Laws in British Colonialism* (New York: Human Rights Watch, 2008), 16.

23 David John Frank, Steven A. Boutcher, and Bayliss Camp, "The Reform of Sodomy Laws: From a World Society Perspective," in *Queer Mobilizations: LGBT Activists Confront the Law*, ed. S. Barclay, M. Berstein, and A. M. Marshall (New York: New York University Press, 2009), 533.

24 Douglas E. Sanders, "377 and the Unnatural Afterlife of British Colonialism in Asia," *Asian Journal of Comparative Law* 4 (2009): 1.

25 Daniel Chernilo, "Social Theory's Methodological Nationalism: Myth and Reality," *European Journal of Social Theory* 9, no. 1 (February 1, 2006): 5–22.
26 Ruth Vanita and Saleem Kidwai, eds., *Same-Sex Love in India: Readings From Literature and History* (New York: Palgrave Macmillan, 2001), xx.
27 Stephen O. Murray, *Homosexualities*, Worlds of Desire (Chicago: University of Chicago Press, 2000).
28 Stephen O. Murray and Will Roscoe, eds., *Boy-Wives and Female Husbands: Studies in African Homosexualities* (New York: Palgrave, 1998), 7.
29 Ibid., 9.
30 Louis Crompton, *Homosexuality and Civilization* (Cambridge, MA: Harvard University Press, 2003), 315–16.
31 Ibid., 240.
32 Wenqing Kang, *Obsession: Male Same-Sex Relations in China, 1900–1950*, Queer Asia (Hong Kong; London: Hong Kong University Press, 2009), 3.
33 Ruth Vanita, "Homosexuality in India: Past and Present," *IIAS Newsletter* (November 1, 2002), 10–11.
34 Ibid.
35 Murray and Roscoe, *Boy-Wives and Female Husbands*, 11.
36 Ibid.

2 The history of British colonialism and the spread of criminal law and penal codes criminalizing homosexuality

The main question we are interested in in this book is whether states' current criminalization of homosexual conduct can be attributed to, or blamed on, the British Empire. But what does it mean to attribute the current law of a sovereign state to an entity that no longer exists? As we will see, there are many different historical processes involved in the British colonial and postcolonial experience, but here we identify several types of situations in which attribution is more or less reasonable.

First, the most common and most clear-cut are cases in which British colonial administrators had formal legal authority over a territory, introduced a law criminalizing homosexual conduct, and that law is still in effect today. Many countries in Asia and Africa, like India, Singapore, Uganda, and Kenya, are these types of cases. Even in this type of situation, the current government bears at least some of the responsibility for the current laws, in that the government could have repealed or replaced the laws. But in addition to the fact of it being an offence at all, the exact wording of the law, the type of offence, and the extent of the penalty, all plausibly might have been different had the British not enacted the law in the first place.

Another set of cases also involves the introduction of British laws or criminal codes that penalized homosexual conduct under colonial rule, and a current law criminalizing homosexual conduct. However, in these cases there was mixed jurisdiction between the British courts and the local courts, and the current law is so dissimilar to the colonial law, for example in wording, or is justified by reference to alternative sources of law, like shari'a law being based on the Qur'an and the Hadith for example, that it seems much less plausible that the current situation is directly attributable to the British Empire. This is the case in the Gulf states of Kuwait, Qatar, and the United Arab Emirates.

Additionally, in a few cases, the British never had formal legal authority over a polity's laws. However, the informal influence, exerted intentionally or not, was such that the laws of that state were borrowed from British exemplars. This is seemingly the case in so-called protected states, like Bhutan, where British control extended only to external affairs and not to domestic politics or legislation. This is similarly the case in colonies that were to a significant extent self-governing, like the primarily white settler colonies of Canada, Australia, and New Zealand.

In this chapter, we do occasionally consider whether a country would have had a law criminalizing homosexual conduct in the counterfactual situation where they had not had their laws determined or influenced by the British Empire. However, the primary purpose of this analysis is to make judgments over the extent to which, in fact, political entities and modern states, in particular, can be said to have had their criminalization law spread to them by the British Empire.

It is convenient to use the term "colonies" for all of the polities that came under some sort of formal British jurisdiction, but there was a wide variety of different arrangements in which British imperial officials had influence of some sort or another. This ranged from quasi-dictatorial powers, through effectively acting only as an appeals court, to unclear personal relationships with the *de jure* ruling person. There is also the issue that there is not a one-to-one correspondence between the administrative boundaries of British Empire polities and current state boundaries. For example, the current West African states of Gambia, Sierra Leone, Ghana, and Nigeria were previously made up of five colonies, four protectorates, and two League of Nations mandates and later trust territories.

An additional complication in attributing current criminalization to the influence of the British Empire is that even though the British may have spread or imposed the law during the colonial period, an entirely separate process brought about the current legal situation. One interesting example is the Sudan, where the version of the criminal code introduced by the British did not in fact criminalize consensual homosexual conduct, although codes introduced subsequent to Sudan's independence did make it illegal.

This chapter is organized primarily around the introduction of several versions of penal or criminal codes and how they spread around the various possessions of the British Empire. First is the Indian penal code (IPC) written by Thomas Macaulay, then a code written by Robert Wright, then a code written by James Fitzjames Stephen, and then a code written by Samuel Griffith for the state of Queensland in Australia, known as the Queensland criminal code (QCC). We also discuss colonies that received other codes or no code at all and instead inherited the common law of England. Finally, we present a timeline of major events in the criminalization and decriminalization of homosexual conduct in the British Empire and in the postcolonial period.

Macaulay's Indian penal code

In 1833, Thomas Babington Macaulay began the job of codifying the law of India, which at that time consisted of "regional regulations, Acts of Parliament, Hindu and Muslim personal law, Islamic criminal law, and the widely interpreted Roman principle of 'justice, equity, and good conscience.'"[1] Part of his reasoning was that the creation of a code would be a "blessing" that the "absolute government" of the British could "confer" on India.[2] His general outlook was that England should act to modernize India, which to him meant Europeanizing or even Anglicizing Indian society.[3] Macaulay produced a criminal code, called the Indian penal code (IPC) in 1837, but it was not adopted until 1860, and while it was originally to come into effect in 1961, it was not implemented until 1862.[4] This code did not encapsulate existing Indian law, but in fact largely reflected a combination of utilitarian-reformist aspirations and laws in force in England. Skuy's analysis reveals that most chapter headings and almost all the offences in the IPC were the same as those in codes that had been drafted in England.[5]

In the 1837 draft, the relevant sections were the following:

> **Unnatural offences**
>
> 361. Whoever, intending to gratify unnatural lust, touches, for that purpose, any person, or any animal, or is by his own consent touched by any person, for the purpose of gratifying unnatural lust, shall be punished with imprisonment of either description for a term which may extend to fourteen years and must not be less than two years, and shall also be liable to fine.
>
> 362. Whoever, intending to gratify unnatural lust, touches for that purpose any person without that person's free and intelligent consent, shall be punished with imprisonment of either description for a term which may extend to life and must not be less than seven years, and shall also be liable to fine.[6]

In a note presented with the 1837 draft, Macaulay elaborated:

> Clause 361 and 362 relate to an odious class of offences respecting which it is desirable that as little as possible should be said. We leave, without comment, to the judgment of his Lordship in Council the two clauses which we have provided for these offences. We are unwilling to insert, either in the text or in the notes, any thing which could give rise to public discussion on this revolting subject; as we are decidedly of opinion that the injury which would be done to the morals of the community by such discussion would far more than compensate for any benefits which might be derived from legislative measures framed with the greatest precision.[7]

After a variety of reconsiderations of many aspects of the IPC by the Indian Law Commission and Supreme Court Judges in Bombay, Calcutta, and Madras, the version that came into force in 1862 contained section 377:

> **Unnatural offences**
>
> 377. Whoever voluntarily has carnal intercourse against the order of nature with any man, woman or animal shall be punished with imprisonment for life, or with imprisonment of either description for a term which may extend to ten years, and shall be liable to fine.
>
> Explanation – Penetration is sufficient to constitute the carnal intercourse necessary to the offence described in this section.

This section remains unchanged today (January 2018). As Gupta notes, there is no distinct criminal offense specifying nonconsensual homosexual conduct (rape was defined in section 375 specifically in terms of a man's rape of a woman), including sex with children.[8] Since 1860, India has become independent from the British Empire and both Pakistan and Bangladesh have become separate independent states. All three have a version of the IPC with an identical section 377, except that Pakistan's section 377 states that the penalty "shall be not less than two years."[9] In 1867, the Straits Settlements went from being administered from India to being a separate crown colony. In 1871, the colony re-enacted the Indian penal code, which had applied previously as the criminal code of the Straits Settlements.[10] Section 377 was included in the code and it followed the evolution of the colony into the modern states of Singapore, Malaysia, and Brunei, with minor variations. In 1886, Burma (Myanmar) became a province of British India and imported the IPC, including section 377. This continued to be the penal code of Myanmar after independence, despite numerous amendments to pre-independence laws.[11]

The mere existence of the Indian penal code made it easier for other jurisdictions to adopt a code, rather than muddle along without a formal codification effort, that is, to retain the English common law. For example, in the colony of Ceylon (Sri Lanka), which adopted a penal code in 1885, "it is safe to say that if these models, which were copied extensively, were not available, the Ceylon codes would not have been enacted."[12] Article 365 of the Ceylon penal code, now the Sri Lankan code, reproduced section 377 of the IPC.[13] Other colonial possessions also used the IPC, including British Somaliland and other protectorates in East Africa, although in many of them it was eventually replaced by other codes (as explained later in the chapter), and in British courts in the Middle East, although it was mostly not adopted in local courts (also discussed later on).

In the existing literature, there is contradictory information available on the Maldives, as noted in Baudh.[14] One source notes that the Maldives Penal Code of 1960 included sections 377C and 377D that criminalized homosexual acts,[15] and Gupta lists the Maldives as inheriting section 377 from the Indian penal code.[16] However, several other sources say that there is no codified prohibition and that the prohibition on homosexual acts in the Maldives prior to 2014 derives from shari'a law.[17] Al Suood (2014) notes that while the penal code adopted in 1961 was based on the Sri Lankan penal code (itself based on the IPC), it "excludes from its purview all criminal offences for which Islamic Shari'ah prescribes punishment."[18] The unofficial English translation of the 1961 penal code only has 166 sections and does not mention any offences related to homosexual conduct.[19]

Another interesting variation on the spread of the IPC and section 377 comes from the Sudan. A penal code modeled on the IPC was introduced into Anglo-Egyptian Sudan in 1899. However, the version of section 377 in this code did not criminalize consensual homosexual acts. Section 318 stated:

> S. 318 Whoever has carnal intercourse against the order of nature with any person without his consent, shall be punished with imprisonment for a term which may extend to fourteen years and shall also be liable to fine; provided that a consent given by a person below the age of sixteen years to such intercourse by his teacher, guardian or any person entrusted with his care or education shall not be deemed to be a consent within the meaning of this section.[20]

In this section, it is only if the carnal intercourse is with a person "without his consent" that it shall be punished. Effectively, then, this code did not criminalize homosexual conduct in Sudan. The penal code was amended in 1924, but "in 1924 anal intercourse between consenting adults was not a crime at all."[21] Subsequent penal codes did criminalize consensual homosexual conduct. The penal code of 1974, enacted after Sudan became independent from the British in 1956, stipulated a prison term of up to two years for both consenting partners and the penal code of 1983 increased the maximum penalty to 14 years.[22] The 1991 Sudanese penal code's provision for sodomy, currently in force, bears no similarity to the wording or framing of either the IPC or the QCC:

> **Section 148. Sodomy**
>
> (1) Any man who inserts his penis or its equivalent into a woman's or a man's anus or permitted another man to insert his penis or its equivalent in his anus is said to have committed Sodomy.

(2) (a) Whoever commits Sodomy shall be punished with flogging one hundred lashes and he shall also be liable to five years imprisonment.
(b) If the offender is convicted for the second time he shall be punished with fogging one hundred lashes and imprisonment for a term which may not exceed five years.
(c) If the offender is convicted for the third time he shall be punished with death or life imprisonment.[23]

Wright's criminal code versus Stephen's criminal code

In 1870, a barrister named Robert S. Wright was tasked by the Colonial Office with composing a criminal code explicitly for the colonies, and Jamaica in particular. In drafting the code, he consulted a variety of existing legal codes including Livingston's 1828 code for Louisiana, Field's New York code, the North German penal code, and others, but Wright was attempting "to reproduce with amendments the English Criminal Law."[24] After Wright submitted his code, James Fitzjames Stephen was asked by the Colonial Office to review the code, which had particular consequences for its treatment of homosexual conduct. Originally, Wright had proposed a maximum two years of penal servitude for an unnatural crime with consent, but Stephen "strongly" dissented and Lord Carnarvon increased the penalty to up to ten years.[25] When the code was finally presented to the UK parliament in 1877, it read as follows:

> **Title XXI, public nuisances**
> **Section 345 public obscenity**
>
> If any two persons are guilty of unnatural connection, or if any person is guilty of unnatural connection with any animal, every such person shall be liable to penal servitude for ten years, and, at the discretion of the court, to flogging or whipping.[26]

There was in the explanatory memorandum, an explanation for why Wright had decreased the penalty compared to the existing ten years to life penal servitude:

> Unnatural crime (without force . . .), is proposed to be removed from the category of crime against which the person, and to be punished under this title, with penal servitude, and flogging or whipping. It is conceived that there is no ground on which the enormous punishment of not less than ten years' penal servitude can be justified where the other party is of an age to consent, and consents; and also that convictions will be more likely to be obtained when a lighter punishment is threatened.[27]

A crucial point to note here is that Wright distinguished between consensual and nonconsensual homosexual conduct. This distinction was absent from the Indian penal code and also from other codes, like Stephen's code and the Queensland criminal code.

Ironically, this code that was called the Jamaica code was not actually brought into force in Jamaica. Initially, the Jamaica Legislative Council passed the Code of Criminal Law (and the Code of Procedure) as initially requested by the Colonial Office in 1879. However, various changes of administration both in London and in the colony of Jamaica brought up concerns about some aspects of the codes and the two codes were eventually repealed in 1889. At around the same time, in 1888, other West Indian colonies, namely British Honduras (Belize) and Tobago adopted the code. British Honduras' criminal code included section 65, which penalized unnatural carnal knowledge by force or without consent with a life sentence (and perhaps flogging), while unnatural connection was a misdemeanor under section 344 punishable with ten years (and perhaps flogging or whipping).[28] However, this retention of Wright's distinction between consensual and nonconsensual acts was removed in a 1944 amendment.[29] Chief Justice John Carrington of St. Lucia obeyed a request from the Colonial Office to draft an "Ordinance in the form of the British Honduras Criminal Code,"[30] which was enacted in 1889. Carrington later became Attorney General of British Guiana (Guyana) from 1889 to 1896 and adopted a similar criminal code in that colony. The criminal code of the colony of the Gold Coast (Ghana), enacted in 1892, was drafted by Sir Joseph Hutchinson and was closely modeled on the 1889 code drafted by the Chief Justice of St. Lucia, which was itself based on Wright's Jamaica code.[31] As with Wright's original code, there was a distinction between consensual and nonconsensual acts, which was carried over to the post-independence era, after 1957, in the 1960 criminal code of Ghana:

Section 104 – unnatural carnal knowledge

(1) Whoever has unnatural carnal knowledge –

(a) of any person of the age of sixteen years or over without his consent shall be guilty of a first-degree felony and shall be liable on conviction to imprisonment for a term of not less than five years and not more than twenty-five years; or

(b) of any person of sixteen years or over with his consent is guilty of a misdemeanour [punishable by up to 3 years imprisonment]; or

(c) of any animal is guilty of a misdemeanour.

(2) Unnatural carnal knowledge is sexual intercourse with a person in an unnatural manner or with an animal.[32]

This code remains in force in Ghana today. Note that the punishment for consensual "unnatural carnal knowledge," as a misdemeanor, is up to three years of imprisonment.

James Fitzjames Stephen, at the request of the Lord Chancellor's Office, drafted his own criminal code, based on his 1874 book *A General View of the Criminal Law of England*, that was published in 1877.[33] This code was then made the basis of an attempted codification of English criminal law, and was introduced to parliament by a royal commission in 1880, although it was never adopted in the United Kingdom. There was a general philosophical difference between the two codes in terms of the relationship between law and morality. As Friedland notes, Wright's code was guided by the sentiment expressed by John Stuart Mill in his seminal work "On Liberty," that "the only purpose for which power can be rightfully exercised over any member of a civilized community, against his will, is to prevent harm to others."[34] By contrast, Stephen was a conservative and a moralistic authoritarian. One difference between the codes was that attempted suicide was not an offense for Wright but it was for Stephen. Wright argued that

> it may be added to the usual arguments based on the absence of injury to any other person, that to impose a punishment for the attempt would be merely to supply an additional motive for taking care to ensure the success of the attempt.[35]

Perhaps in keeping with his harsher and more traditional moralism, Stephen's code included the following articles:

> **Unnatural offence**
>
> 140. Every one is guilty of a crime and liable to *penal servitude for life* who commits buggery either with a human being or with any other living creature.
>
> **Attempt to commit unnatural offence**
>
> 141. Every one is guilty of a crime and liable to *ten years' penal servitude* who attempts to commit buggery, or who being a male indecently assaults any other male.[36]

Notice that, whereas Wright's code was amended (partly by Stephen) to increase the penalty for consensual "unnatural connection" to ten years penal servitude, Stephen's code mandates a life sentence. In addition, just one more of the implications of this framing that appears perverse to modern eyes is that, taken together, these articles, 140 and 141, seem to mean that given a choice between claiming consensual homosexual sex (i.e. "buggery") and sexual assault of a male that did not rise to the level of "buggery," a defendant would be better off pretending to have committed near-rape.

Stephen's code was influential in a particular way and was instrumental in the form that criminalization of homosexual conduct took in some British colonies. In addition to what might be called the "imposed" imperial codes that British colonial administrations drafted and enacted, there were also efforts by "self-governing" colonies towards criminal law codification. The three main examples are the Canadian (1892), New Zealand (1893), and Australian (primarily Queensland 1899) codes.[37]

These self-governed codes were relatively democratic and autonomous in the sense that they were based on an exemplar from Britain, namely Stephen's draft code, but combined it with local considerations in voluntary legislative processes. Codification efforts that failed in England, perhaps partly because of entrenched interests in maintaining the existing common law system, were more popular in colonial settings. In addition, whereas Macaulay's IPC and Wright's Jamaica code carried the association of being intended for non-white native subject peoples, Stephen's draft code nearly became domestic English law in 1880. Both the Canadian and New Zealand codes were consciously modeled on Stephen's code.

Canada was the first self-governing jurisdiction in the British Empire to enact a criminal code in 1892. Previously, there had been no federal criminal law in the territory, although English public and criminal law had been in effect in Upper Canada (Ontario) since 1792. George Burbidge, the deputy minister of justice, Robert Sedgewick, and John Thompson, justice minister, drafted the bill while being advised by Judge James Gowan, who had been in London while Stephen's draft code was debated.[38] The primary references they used were the Stephen's code as manifested in the 1880 English parliamentary bill and some existing Canadian statutes, as well as other more minor references.[39] The resulting code, passed by the legislature in June 1892, is very similar to Stephen's code in many respects and includes the following articles:

Unnatural offence

174. Every one is guilty of an indictable offence and liable to imprisonment for life who commits buggery, either with a human being or with any other living creature.

Attempt to commit sodomy

175. Every one is guilty of an indictable offence and liable to ten years' imprisonment who attempts to commit the offence mentioned in the next preceding section.[40]

While it began its attempts at codification sooner, introducing a government bill in 1883, New Zealand's Criminal Code Act only became law in 1893. Alexander Johnstone, a Supreme Court judge and Walter Reid, the solicitor general, were tasked with preparing a criminal code for New Zealand in 1878 and they worked primarily from Stephen's draft code (and the 1880 bill), to the extent that the final text of the 1883 code introduced to parliament included a memorandum and notes that explained the advantages of using Stephen's code.[41] After a decade of various political issues, the code was passed in 1893, and included the following articles:

Unnatural offence

136. (1) Every one is liable to imprisonment with hard labour for life, and, according to his age, to be flogged or whipped once, twice, or thrice, who commits buggery either with a human being or with any other living creature.
(2) This offence is complete upon penetration.

Attempt to commit unnatural offence

137. Every one is liable to ten years' imprisonment with hard labour, and according to his age, to be flogged or whipped once, twice, or thrice, who –

(1) Attempts to commit buggery; or
(2) Assaults any person with intent to commit buggery; or
(3) Who being a male indecently assaults any other male.

It shall be no defence to an indictment for an indecent assault on a male of any age that he consented to the act of indecency.[42]

Notice that both the Canadian and the New Zealand articles are very similar to those from Stephen's code as they appeared to the UK parliament in 1880. Stephen uses the word buggery but labels the article "unnatural offence," as does the New Zealand code, while the Canadian code uses the word sodomy in the article criminalizing attempts. The New Zealand code is more specific, including a definition in subsection 2 ("penetration," although of what and by what is left unsaid) and also specifies that consent is no defense against being charged with indecent assault. Regardless of these minor modifications, there can be no doubt that the form of the articles and the level of punishment were strongly if not decisively influenced by Stephen's code.

The Queensland criminal code

Samuel Griffith, though born in Wales, was premier of Queensland from 1883 to 1888 and 1890 to 1893 and then chief justice of Queensland from 1893 to 1903. He was responsible for several pieces of criminal justice legislation, including the Justices Act of 1886 and the Offenders Probation Act of 1886. When he was an undergraduate student at the University of Sydney, he won a scholarship to travel to Europe where he learned Italian, which turned out to be relevant to his being able to use the Italian Penal Code of 1888/9 as a source for the Queensland criminal code. Griffith began work on the criminal code in 1896 and in order to do so, read copies of the criminal law of many countries. His first draft of 1897 was accompanied by an explanatory letter, in which he noted that he had derived assistance from an English draft code of criminal law (i.e., Stephen's code), but that this code had some problems. He also said that he had very great assistance from the 1888 Italian Penal Code, known as the Zardanelli code after the Italian justice minister associated with it. Griffith called this Italian code "the most complete and perfect Penal Code in existence."[43] His draft code was presented to the Criminal Code Commission in Queensland in 1899 and after a few modifications it was passed that year. It included section 208:

> **Unnatural offences**
>
> 208. Any Person who –
>
> (1) Has carnal knowledge of any person against the order of nature; or
> (2) Has carnal knowledge of an animal; or
> (3) Permits a male person to have carnal knowledge of him or her against the order of nature;
>
> is guilty of a crime, and is liable to imprisonment with hard labour for fourteen years.
>
> **Attempt to commit unnatural offences**
>
> 209. Any person who attempts to commit any of the crimes defined in the last preceding section is guilty of a crime, and is liable to imprisonment with hard labour for seven years. The offender cannot be arrested without warrant.[44]

The migration of the Griffith code (QCC)

While Sir Samuel Griffith was engaged in drafting his criminal code, he sent copies to various other colonial officials, lawyers, and politicians in other colonies in Australia. Only three other Australian states ever codified their criminal law, all three were to some extent based on the QCC, but it seems reasonable that the criminalization of homosexual conduct was specifically a product of the QCC in Western Australia and Tasmania. Western Australia codified their criminal law by adopting the Griffith code with minor amendments in 1902. Legislative discussion at the time indicates that the main reason for adopting a criminal code was to have local legislation accessible to all, rather than common law based on English statutes.[45] The code included the following sections:

> **Unnatural offences**
>
> 181. ANY person who –
>
> (1) Has carnal knowledge of any person against the order of nature: or
> (2) Has carnal knowledge of an animal; or
> (3) Permits a male person to have carnal knowledge of him or her against the order of nature:
>
> is guilty of a crime, and is liable to imprisonment with hard labour for fourteen years, with or without whipping.
>
> **Attempt to commit unnatural offences**
>
> 182. ANY person who attempts to commit any of the crimes defined in the last preceding section is guilty of a crime, and is liable to imprisonment with hard labour for seven years, with or without whipping. The offender cannot be arrested without warrant.[46]

As can be seen, the only difference from the QCC is the provision that whipping is an option.

When Tasmania was considering adopting a criminal code in 1924, after a draft had been prepared by Justice Ewing, a supreme court judge, the attorney general Albert Ogilvie specifically addressed its influences:

> In the framing of the Code, while the draft prepared some years ago by Mr Justice Ewing, and the Queensland Code, have been followed to a great extent, the draftsmen have drawn freely upon the Draft Code of 1879 prepared by the Criminal Code Commissioners appointed in England for that purpose, and upon legislation recently passed in England to simplify and consolidate portions of the criminal law.[47]

However, section 122 of the Tasmania Criminal Code Act of 1924 was identical to article 208 of the QCC. The language of "carnal knowledge" was amended in 1984 to "sexual intercourse" but Tasmania did not repeal this section until 1997.[48]

In addition to its use in Australia, the QCC was also the source of laws criminalizing homosexual conduct in several states and islands in the Pacific. In 1888, under pressure from the colony of Queensland, the British annexed British New Guinea (later Papua) and adopted English common law and Queensland-based statutes. After the Griffith code came into force in Queensland in 1901, British New Guinea adopted the code in 1902 as The Criminal Code Ordinance of 1902. German New Guinea was occupied by Australian forces during World War I and was subsequently allocated by the League of Nations as a mandate to the British Crown administered by the Australian government. In 1921, the governor general adopted the Laws Repeal and Adopting Ordinance, repealing the German laws and adopting, among others, the Griffith code.[49] The 1974 criminal code includes section 210, which is the same as the QCC's 208, except for replacing "has carnal knowledge of" with "sexually penetrates."[50]

In 1920, Nauru was allocated as a League of Nations mandate to the United Kingdom, Australia, and New Zealand. In 1921, the QCC was adopted in Nauru.[51] In May 2016, the Crimes Act 2016 repealed previous criminal laws. The government of Nauru stated that this law removed homosexuality as an offence.[52]

In the colony of Fiji, the penal code of 1945 was based on the QCC[53] and included section 175:

> **Unnatural offences**
>
> 175. Any person who –
>
> (a) has carnal knowledge of any person against the order of nature; or
> (b) has carnal knowledge of an animal; or
> (c) permits a male person to have carnal knowledge of him or her against the order of nature, is guilty of a felony, and is liable to imprisonment for fourteen years, with or without corporal punishment.

However, enforcement in Fiji of this and the law against "committing acts of gross indecency with other male persons" was adjusted to local conditions, as can be seen in the case of *R v. Vodo Vuli* when a sentence was reduced from 30 to 12 months because "The offender had apologised to the boys' parents and made traditional Fijian peace to them by presenting a whale's tooth."[54]

The British Solomon Islands Protectorate adopted a penal code in 1963 that was also "virtually . . . identical" to the QCC.[55] Both Tuvalu and Kiribati were part of the Gilbert and Ellice Islands Protectorate until the mid-1970s with Tuvalu becoming a separate dependency in 1975 and then becoming independent in 1978 and Kiribati becoming the independent Republic of Kiribati in 1979. Both countries have a mix of British common law and retain the 1965 penal code enacted while a protectorate. This penal code includes the following article:

> **153. Unnatural offences**
>
> Any person who – (a) commits buggery with another person or with an animal; or (b) permits a male person to commit buggery with him or her, shall be guilty of a felony, and shall be liable to imprisonment for 14 years.

Further afield, after Griffith's QCC had been adopted in Northern Nigeria (discussed in more detail later in the chapter), the island of Bermuda, under British rule since 1684, adopted a criminal code in 1907 that included section 179, largely reproducing section 208 of the QCC. This was amended in 1994 by adding a subsection such that buggery "shall not constitute an offence if committed in private by two consenting persons both above the age of eighteen years."[56]

The history of criminal law codification in Nigeria is more convoluted than many others covered in this chapter. In September 1889, a dispute over the distinction between "hard labour" and "penal servitude" led to an invitation to adopt Wright's Jamaica code by the Colonial Office to the Governors of Lagos, the Gold Coast, Sierra Leone, and the Gambia. Only the Gold Coast did so (discussed in the preceding paragraphs). In 1898, the new governor of Lagos wrote to the colonial secretary opining "what a convenience it would be were Ordinances similar to the Penal Code and the Summary Jurisdiction Ordinance of the Straits Settlements introduced in the Colony."[57] In fact, an 1899 bill introducing a code written by Queen's Advocate Edlin based on the Gold Coast code was withdrawn in the face of resistance in the legislative council.

In Northern Nigeria, a different colony (or rather, protectorate) from Lagos, a draft criminal code was written by Chief Justice Henry C. Gollan. After he considered the Gold Coast code, Stephen's code, the 1899 Sudan penal code, and the Indian penal code, he decided to adopt the QCC, providing his reasoning as follows:

> My principal reasons for coming to this conclusion were that the Queensland Code appeared to me to keep in a much more satisfactory manner than any of the other Codes I have mentioned the mean between over elaboration on the one hand and over compression on the other; and avoided what seems to me to be the fault in particular of the

> Gold Coast Code, the relegation to definition sections of practically all the essential features of the offences constituted under its provisions.[58]

He thought it would be hard to use by officials with no legal training. There is no mention of anything substantive about the nature of the offences or the types or amounts of punishment. An interesting counterfactual is, if Gollan had adopted the Gold Coast code with its distinction between consensual and nonconsensual "unnatural carnal knowledge" and lesser classification, or even the Sudan penal code with its lack of criminalization of consensual homosexual acts, whether those elements would have been copied by all of the later criminal codes that used the Nigerian code as a basis.

The protectorate of Southern Nigeria, despite much discussion amongst officials of the Colonial Office, did not end up receiving a criminal code, but after the amalgamation of Northern and Southern Nigeria into a single protectorate the code in force in the north was extended over the entire territory in 1916. This Nigerian criminal code of 1916 ended up becoming the basis for a wide variety of other codes around the British Empire, spreading the QCC and its version of the criminalization of homosexual conduct far and wide.

East Africa and the transition from IPC to QCC

There were several phases in which the criminal laws of British East Africa were imposed on the colonies by the colonial authorities. First, in a series of decisions to adopt the laws or codes that were operative in India at that time, the Indian penal code was taken as authoritative in the territories that eventually became the modern states of Tanzania, Kenya, Uganda, Malawi, and Zambia. These arrangements then faced a series of pressures, such as from white settler colonials who objected to being subject to laws intended for native subject peoples rather than English law, as well as the feelings of legal advisors in the Colonial Office that some of the provisions of the IPC were too far removed from those current in English domestic law.

The first place where the IPC was formally applied to an East African territory was Zanzibar in 1867, initially through a regulation made by the British consul there, which was confirmed by the Zanzibar (Indian penal code) Order in Council of 1882. In 1897, the East Africa Order in Council replaced the previous laws with various Indian acts including the IPC in the East Africa Protectorate (later the colony and protectorate of Kenya). In 1900, the IPC was applied to the "railway zone" in Uganda's eastern province, followed by the 1902 Uganda Order in Council that stated that jurisdiction in the entire territory should be exercised in conformity with the penal code of India. After the World War I, the mandate of Tanganyika was allocated to Britain under the League of Nations mandate system and various Indian acts, including the Indian penal code, were applied under the Indian Acts (Application) Ordinance of 1920.[59]

In 1925, the parliamentary undersecretary of state for the colonies, William Ormsby-Gore, decided that a new criminal code should be drafted in the Colonial Office and applied to the three East African territories and Nyasaland (Malawi), overriding dissent from the authorities in the colonies themselves.[60] Albert Ehrhardt, a temporary assistant legal advisor, drafted a model penal code based on the Nigerian criminal code of 1916 (itself based on the Queensland criminal code of 1899, described earlier). William MacGregor had taken a physical copy of the Queensland code to Lagos where it had a decisive influence on Ehrhardt.[61] This model penal code was then sent to the colonies, where it was very unpopular among the British colonial and legal authorities there, such as at the Conference of East African Law Officers where objections were raised to the fact that they would have to go through the effort to learn a new code and set of precedents.[62] Regardless of this opposition, the Colonial Office insisted that the new code be adopted and in 1930, Kenya, Uganda, Tanganyika, and Nyasaland all enacted a penal code based on the model penal code. The Northern Rhodesian (Zambia) penal code was enacted in 1931, but Zanzibar was not forced to abandon its existing IPC-based code until 1934, along with the Gambia.[63]

Bechuanaland (Botswana) became a British protectorate in 1885. Common law was immediately introduced, such that "the law to be administered shall, as nearly as the circumstances of the country will permit, be the same as the law for the time being in force in Colony of the Cape of Good Hope," that is, initially Roman-Dutch common law but by the late 19th century, substantially modified by English law.[64] In 1964, a penal code was introduced that was based on penal codes from East and Central African countries, themselves based on the Colonial Office model code, based on the Nigerian criminal code, based on the QCC. Keeping in mind that the draftsman of the Botswana code aimed to avoid undue conflict with the existing Cape colonial civil law, the code was "founded largely, though not exclusively on English law rather than Cape Colonial law."[65] This 1964 penal code included these sections:

164. Unnatural offences

Any person who –

(a) has carnal knowledge of any person against the order of nature; or
(b) has carnal knowledge of an animal; or
(c) permits a male person to have carnal knowledge of him or her against the order of nature; is guilty of an offence and is liable to imprisonment for a term not exceeding seven years.

> **165. Attempt to commit unnatural offences**
>
> Any person who attempts to commit any of the offences specified in section 164 is guilty of an offence and is liable to imprisonment for a term not exceeding five years.[66]

These are the same as 208 and 209 of the QCC, except that seven years (and five for attempted) is a lighter sentence. Botswana became independent in 1966 and retained the code in its entirety and it is still in force. A 1998 Penal Code Amendment Act changed the language of section 164 from "a male" to "any" to include sexual acts between women.[67]

British Middle East and Arabian Gulf

Perhaps the most surprising stories of colonial status and current laws criminalizing homosexual conduct are those that come from the Middle East and the Arabian Gulf in particular. If we were to look only at the broad categories of colonial heritage and current criminalization, we would miss a good part of the processes that actually transpired in those states. Some states that are widely considered to have once been British colonies, like Egypt or the United Arab Emirates, did not inherit their legal systems, not to mention their laws on homosexual conduct, from the British Empire. One state that was not technically a British colony, Israel, did in fact directly inherit its law criminalizing homosexual conduct as a result of British imperial imposition.

After World War I, the supreme commander of the British forces of occupation in Iraq drew up the penal code that became the Baghdad penal code of 1919. This code did address sodomy in article 232, but only sodomy without consent or on a child of 15 years or less.[68] The United Kingdom was allocated Iraq (or Mesopotamia) as a mandate by the League of Nations, although this was only enacted in 1922 after a violent revolt against proposed British rule was defeated and a treaty was signed between the British and the kingdom of Iraq. While nominally independent in domestic affairs, Iraq was under the influence of the British until the end of the mandate, when Iraq became fully sovereign in 1932. Schmitt and Sofer report that sodomy was criminalized in the 1969 penal code, with a maximum penalty of 15 years in article 393.[69] However, article 393 reads:

> Article 393 – (1) Any person who has sexual intercourse with a female without her consent or commits buggery with any person without their consent is punishable by a term of imprisonment not exceeding 15 years.[70]

Again, only sodomy without consent is punishable. Despite conflicting reports, the Global Justice Project Iraq states that officially homosexuality has never been illegal in Iraq, and definitely since 2003, when the coalitional provisional authority re-instituted the 1969 penal code, homosexual conduct has not been criminalized.[71]

Schmitt and Sofer write that in 1956, the IPC "was replaced in the British territories of the Persian Gulf by a new Penal Code. Article 171 made sodomy punishable by imprisonment not exceeding 10 years, with or without corporal punishment."[72] However, this story is too simplistic and is in fact misleading. All of the Arab states of the Gulf region – Bahrain, the Trucial States (now the United Arab Emirates), Kuwait, and Qatar – reached agreements in which they ceded control over their external affairs to the British Empire, while leaving domestic jurisdiction untouched. However, a mixture of British mistrust of local legal systems, based partly on shari'a, and the idea within Islam that non-Muslims were subject to their own laws, led to local rulers granting authority over most foreigners to British-administered courts. There was little conflict over these issues, primarily because there was so little activity, until after Indian independence in 1947, when the Foreign Office took control of the Gulf from the India Office. At that time there were more Gulf residents under British jurisdiction, and large-scale oil production started to become a serious prospect. So, in the 1950s and 1960s, the British started to aim at developing the Gulf legal systems along British lines.

The centerpiece of these efforts was a new British-authored law code. In 1956 a writer could still comment that "The law applied by the British courts in the Persian Gulf still is based to a considerable extent on Indian codes in the form which they had on August 14, 1947."[73] However, the IPC was felt to be outdated and complex, and British common law was felt to be unappealing to the local inhabitants, and so the new law code was aimed at suiting the local conditions. The goal was to promulgate the code for the British courts and to induce local rulers to adopt it for their courts too.

British influence was greatest in Bahrain and it was there that they tried to introduce the new draft penal code, which was ready in 1954. The amir of Bahrain agreed to adopt the code simultaneously with the British after minor modifications. However, there was such a backlash against this foreign imposition, which included criminalizing offences against the Queen and the British government, that it was suspended. In order to use the sections on sedition, association, and assembly against the political opposition, the amir enacted the code in November 1956, with the British following suit in their courts in Bahrain.[74]

The Foreign Office had the code come into force in all British courts outside Bahrain in 1956. The son of the Kuwaiti amir, and the commander of the police, as well as other Kuwaiti officials asked for a copy of the code in 1955 but rejected it in 1956. By 1957, the Foreign Office had given up the idea of trying to get local rulers to adopt the British code. For example, as Brown notes, "by the time Kuwait gained independence in 1961, there were only a few traces of British legal influence."[75]

The 1956 model penal code introduced in Bahrain was based on the Sudanese penal code that had already been referred to by Bahrain courts.[76] Perhaps ironically, Bahrain, the only Gulf state where the British penal code, including article 171 criminalizing homosexual conduct, was implemented, is also the only one that has since decriminalized homosexual conduct. In 1976, Bahrain's current penal code was enacted, which decriminalized consensual adult same-sex sexual behavior, while keeping the age of consent at 21 years, one year higher for same-sex sexual acts than for heterosexual acts.[77]

Palestine, Cyprus, and Israel

During World War I, the British occupied Palestine as well as the territory of Transjordan, which were both allocated to Britain under the League of Nations British Mandate for Palestine in 1922. Under the mandate, the British had responsibility for military, political, legal, and administrative control, which lay with the Colonial Office. Before the British administration, the Ottoman penal code did not criminalize consensual homosexual acts. However, in 1936, the mandate authorities outlawed consensual homosexual relations between adults in the Palestine Criminal Code Ordinance (PCCO). Sir Michael McDonnell, chief justice of the Supreme Court of Palestine consulted with the attorney general and they together approached the high commissioner and suggested that Palestine should have a code based on the 1928 Cyprus code.[78] There were two relevant sections of the PCCO. First, section 152(1) punished sodomy committed on a person against his will, by the use of force or threats of death or severe bodily harm, on a person who was unconscious or unable to resist, or with a child under the age of 16, regardless of consent or the absence of force.[79] Section 152(2) of the PCCO criminalized consensual homosexual acts.

> The *Palestine Criminal Code Ordinance* of 1936 thus may fairly be described as a direct descendant of the Queensland Criminal Code of 1899 and a closely related cousin to numerous Criminal Codes promulgated by the British in colonial East Africa and elsewhere.[80]

The basis of the PCCO was the Cyprus Criminal Code Order of 1928 that was based on the criminal code of Nigeria, which was based on the QCC. Section 152(2) of the PCCO was a replica of section 208 of the QPC (although with only ten years' imprisonment as the maximum penalty rather than 14).

Subsequently, some of the territory of the British Mandate for Palestine became the State of Israel as a result of the success of the Israeli independence movement in the Arab-Israeli war of 1948. The 1936 PCCO continued to apply in the new state.[81] In 1977 a new penal law[82] was enacted that included section 351, labeled Deviations from the Order of Nature:

> A person who does one of the following is liable to imprisonment for ten years:
>
> (1) Has carnal knowledge of a person against the order of nature;
> (2) has carnal knowledge of an animal;
> (3) permits a male person to have carnal knowledge of him;
> (4) permits a male person to have carnal knowledge of her against the order of nature.

This reproduces the wording of the PCCO. However, this section was repealed in 1988.

Southern Africa

Despite the fact that South Africa was a British colony for over 100 years, it is somewhat problematic to attribute the criminalization of homosexual conduct in South Africa to the British. Prior to British rule, the Cape of Good Hope was settled by colonists from the Netherlands, who brought what is known as Roman-Dutch law with them. This included various relevant offences, including "sodomie," which was used to mean many types of acts in addition to male-to-male sexual conduct, like masturbation or fellatio.[83] England annexed the Cape of Good Hope during the Napoleonic wars in 1806. The Napoleonic code decriminalizing all same-sex sexual acts was spread throughout the French Empire, now including the Netherlands, and presumably would have applied in the Cape colony, too. However, as the territory was now under British control, there was no change in the previous criminalization. Sodomy remained an offence under South African common law throughout British rule and beyond.

Under the South Africa Act of 1909, South Africa became the Union of South Africa, consisting of the Cape colony, the colony of Natal, the Transvaal colony, and the Orange River colony. Though a British governor general, and the British monarch, had ultimate executive power, the local South African government composed of a parliament and a prime minister, had much independence. During this period, the League of Nations awarded the mandate of South West Africa (Namibia), a former German colony, to South Africa. South Africa then brought their existing legal system into the territory, including the common law offense of sodomy as well as "unnatural offences."[84] The spread of criminalization to modern Namibia thus is not as direct a result of British imperial rule as some other countries. However, it is possible either that had South Africa not had mandatory power over Southwest Africa, or if South African common law had not criminalized homosexual conduct, then Namibia would not today consider it an offence.

Another implication of South Africa's criminalization was the effect on Zimbabwe's laws. Cecil Rhodes formed the British South Africa Company in 1889 in order to establish rule over territories in Matabeleland, Mashonaland, among others. After the first Matabele war, Rhodes also gained control of all the territory between the Limpopo River and Lake Tanganyika. These territories were formed into Southern Rhodesia (now Zimbabwe) and Northern Rhodesia (now Zambia). Formal control of these territories reverted to the United Kingdom in 1923.

Southern Rhodesia never codified its criminal law under British rule, but the common law first introduced by Cecil Rhodes' British South Africa Company did mean that same-sex sexual conduct was criminalized throughout British rule and after independence. Zimbabwe introduced a Criminal Law (Codification and Reform) Act in 2006, section 73 of which does not read similarly to any of the codes considered in this chapter, and in fact includes a penalty of "a fine up to or exceeding level fourteen or imprisonment for a period not exceeding one year or both," which is considerably more lenient than many other countries.[85] By contrast, in 1930, Northern Rhodesia adopted a new penal code, and in 1933 adopted Act No. 26, which created sections 155 through 158.[86] Sections 155 and 156 are the same as sections 208 and 209 of the QCC. These sections remained identical after independence from Britain in 1964 and today the only amendment was to increase the penalty from up to fourteen years to "not less than fifteen years."[87]

Swaziland, previously a protectorate of the Boer South African Republic, came under direct British rule as a protectorate in 1906. Common law was introduced into the territory. From 1939, the Criminal Law and Procedure Act included section 185(5), which states that "Any person charged with sodomy or assault with the intent to commit sodomy may be found guilty of indecent assault or common assault, if such be the facts proved."[88] Same-sex sexual relations remains a common law offence today.[89] Basutoland (Lesotho) was brought under the direct authority of Queen Victoria and her high commissioner in 1871 and British common law gradually became part of the legal landscape, including the prohibition on sodomy.[90] The 1938 Criminal Procedure and Evidence Act was the same as that of Swaziland.[91] However, in 2010, a new penal code act was adopted and article 52 "erases the punitive enumeration of [male] sodomy indicated" in the existing legislation.[92]

The common law and criminalization without codes

In the United Kingdom, the Offences Against the Person Act (OATPA) was passed in 1861; it included section 61, Sodomy and Bestiality:

> Whosoever shall be convicted of the abominable Crime of Buggery, committed either with Mankind or with any Animal, shall be liable, at the Discretion of the Court, to be kept in Penal Servitude for Life or for any Term not less than Ten Years.[93]

Versions of this section were authoritative in many British colonial possessions, including some Australian states like New South Wales, Hong Kong, Sierra Leone, Swaziland, Trinidad and Tobago, Jamaica, the Bahamas, Antigua and Barbuda, and St. Kitts and Nevis. As common law countries, they had a variety of sources of law, but all of them in some way referred back to the United Kingdom's Offences Against the Person Act 1861. So, while there was no local codification of criminal law as there was in other possessions, the source of the current criminalization was originally the British legal system. Jamaica enacted its own version of the Offences Against the Person Act in 1864, which included a lesser penalty of "a term not exceeding ten years."[94] As was the case in several countries, the Bahamas retained the 1861 law even though it obtained independence in 1973, which was after the repeal of the buggery law in England and Wales in 1967.[95]

Indirect British influence and criminalization

The history of several other modern states has included very close relations with the British Empire, or at least its representatives, without it being reasonable to attribute their adoption of a law criminalizing homosexuality to direct British influence. For example, Tonga was never formally under British rule but was a "protected state," meaning domestic independence but control over foreign affairs, from 1900 to 1970. Western Samoa was a New Zealand League Mandate, and previously a German colony, so it seems a stretch to blame the British, especially as the Samoan law bears no particular resemblance to any of the codes considered in this analysis.[96] The British did not have control over Bhutan's internal administration and anyway renounced their previous relationship after Indian independence in 1947. Bhutan's criminal code, part of the Thrimzhung Chenmo (supreme law) was enacted in the 1950s, after any formal British influence had ended.[97] That said, it cannot be a coincidence that Bhutan's penal code of 2004 includes article 213:

> Unnatural Sex: A defendant shall be guilty of the offence of unnatural sex, if the defendant engages in sodomy or any other sexual conduct

that is against the order of nature (although this is classed as a "petty misdemeanor" with a penalty of less than one year).[98]

Conclusion

In contrast with the British experience, the other big colonial power – France – did not leave such an institutional legacy on the criminalization of homosexual conduct. Due to developments in Enlightenment concepts of liberty and rights after the French Revolution, the French penal code of 1791 decriminalized sodomy between overage consenting adults in private. This code was subsequently spread by Napoleon's conquests in continental Europe and through the French Empire.[99]

As was mentioned earlier in this chapter, we do not aim to make detailed causal claims for all of the countries and former colonies discussed. However, we can use the evidence herein to make some interesting comparisons. For example, look at the current legal situation in former British African colonies in Table 2.1. We can see that there is a clear difference between the current penalties for what is called buggery or carnal knowledge against the order of nature in the countries that inherited a version of the QCC or the Offences Against the Person Act of 1861, with their harsh penalties and lack of a distinction between consensual and nonconsensual homosexual sex, and Ghana, the only African country to have its criminal code based on Wright's code from 1877. Ghana's current code not only distinguishes between acts with and without consent, as did Wright in 1877, but also classes unnatural carnal knowledge with consent as a misdemeanor, which is analogous to Wright's classification of it as only a public nuisance. While not dispositive, as there are potentially other relevant omitted variables that could explain this difference, it seems plausible that the reason why there is this current difference in the legal treatment of homosexual conduct is

Table 2.1 Current laws in selected former British colonies in Africa

State	*Max penalty*	*Classification*	*Origin*
Ghana	3 years	Misdemeanor	Wright's code
Kenya	7–14 years	Felony	QCC
Uganda	Life	Felony	QCC
Nigeria	14 years	Felony	QCC
Gambia	14 years	Felony	QCC
Zambia	>15 years to life	Felony	QCC
Botswana	7 years	–	QCC
Sierra Leone	>10 years to life	–	OATPA 1861

All penalties and classifications from Carroll and Mendos, "State-Sponsored Homophobia" the origin of the criminal law in the particular criminal code introduced by British colonial administrators.

Perhaps a similar dynamic explains the situation in Iraq; despite Iraq being a nation surrounded by states criminalizing homosexual conduct and being almost entirely Muslim, the Iraq penal code of 1969 does not prohibit same-sex relations.[100] The British-imposed Baghdad penal code of 1919 only criminalized sodomy without consent.

This chapter has shown that the legacy of British colonialism on the legal classification of homosexual conduct was strong and widespread but also more complicated than a simple narrative of imposition. Some modern states did have their laws imposed on them by the British. Other states copied verbatim, or near verbatim, British exemplars of criminal laws and codes. But some other states, despite their experiences with British imperialism, did not receive their laws criminalizing homosexual conduct from the British and are wholly responsible for them. In the next chapter, we systematically address whether former British colonies are in fact more likely to have these laws than former colonies of other European powers, and also whether it has been harder for former British colonies to rid themselves of this legacy.

Timeline of criminalization and decriminalization

1534 – Legal statute under Henry VIII takes over the offence of "vice of buggery" from ecclesiastical law, with the death penalty.

1837 – Thomas Babington Macaulay drafts version of Indian penal code.

1861 – Offences Against the Person Act (UK) includes the offense of "buggery," with the penalty being ten years in prison.

1862 – Indian penal code, including section 377 with punishment for life or ten years, comes into force.

1865 – Hong Kong adopts Offences Against the Person Act.

1867 – Indian penal code applied to Zanzibar (Tanzania) by British Consul.

1871 – Straits Settlement Law (covering Singapore, Malaysia, and Brunei, and based on IPC), including section 377, enacted.

1877 – Robert S. Wright drafts a criminal code for Jamaica, with buggery as a "public nuisance" with a maximum penalty of two years imprisonment, which is, in the end, not adopted in Jamaica.

1878 – James Fitzjames Stephen's English draft code, including minimum ten-year sentence for buggery, introduced into UK parliament (and in 1879 and 1880) but was not adopted.

1885 – A penal code was introduced in Ceylon (Sri Lanka) based on the IPC.

1888 – British Honduras (Belize) adopts Wright's code.

1892 – Canada criminal code, largely copied from Stephen's code and including sections 174 and 175, was adopted.
The colony of the Gold Coast (Ghana) adopts a new criminal code based on Wright's Jamaica code.
1893 – New Zealand Criminal Code Act, including sections 136 and 137, based on Stephen's code, enacted.
1897 – East Africa Protectorate (Kenya) applies IPC.
1899 – Queensland criminal code, including section 208, drafted by Sir Samuel Griffith.
1899 – Sudanese penal code, including section 318, based on IPC, adopted.[101]
1900 – New South Wales enacts Crimes Act, including section 79.
1901 – Queensland criminal code comes into force.
1902 – Uganda applies IPC.
1903 – Criminal code applied in Papua (Papua New Guinea), based on QCC.
1904 – Northern Nigeria criminal code comes into force (based on QCC).
1907 – Bermuda adopts penal code (based on QCC).
1916 – After amalgamation of Southern and Northern Nigeria (1914), whole of Nigeria adopts criminal code based on QCC.
1920 – Tanganyika (Tanzania) applies IPC.
1921 – Criminal code based on QCC introduced to British New Guinea (Papua New Guinea).
QCC is introduced to Nauru.
1924 – Tasmania adopts Criminal Code Act based on QCC.
1929 – Cyprus criminal code, including section 171, enacted (based on QCC).
1930 – Kenya, Uganda, Tanganyika (Tanzania), and Nyasaland (Malawi) adopt new penal codes based on the 1916 Nigerian code (based on the QCC).
1931 – Northern Rhodesia (Zambia) adopts penal code based on QCC.
1934 – Criminal Code of the Gambia enacted, based on QCC.
Zanzibar enacts a penal decree based on the Kenya penal code (based on the QCC).
1936 – Consensual homosexual sex criminalized in the British Mandate of Palestine.
1945 – Fiji's new penal code includes section 175, criminalizing homosexual conduct.
1955 – Seychelles penal code comes into force, based on QCC.
1956 – New penal codes (replacing the IPC) for British courts in Aden (Yemen), Kuwait, Muscat and Oman (Oman), Qatar, and the Trucial States (United Arab Emirates), and in both British and

local courts in Bahrain, include article 171 in which sodomy is punishable by up to ten years' imprisonment.

1957 – Wolfenden Report (UK) urges that "homosexual behaviour between consenting adults in private should no longer be a criminal offence."

1963 – Solomon Islands Protectorate adopts penal code based on QCC.

1964 – Bechuanaland Protectorate (Botswana) adopts penal code, including section 164, based on the QCC.

1967 – England and Wales decriminalize most consensual homosexual conduct.

1970 – Canada decriminalizes homosexual conduct.

1975 – South Australia decriminalizes homosexual conduct.

1976 – Australian Capital Territory decriminalizes homosexual conduct.

1980 – Scotland decriminalizes homosexual conduct.

1981 – Victoria decriminalizes homosexual conduct.

1982 – UK parliament extends decriminalization to Northern Ireland.

1984 – Northern Territory decriminalizes homosexual conduct.
New South Wales decriminalizes homosexual conduct.

1990 – Hong Kong decriminalizes consensual homosexual sex.
Western Australia decriminalizes homosexual conduct.

1991 – Queensland decriminalizes homosexual conduct.

1991 – The Bahamas removes prohibitions against buggery and lesbianism in private.

1993 – Ireland decriminalizes homosexual conduct.

1994 – Australian parliament enacts Human Rights (sexual conduct) Act, making it illegal to criminalize sexual conduct between consenting adults acting in private.

Bermuda passes a Criminal Code Amendment Act decriminalizing homosexual conduct.

1997 – Tasmania decriminalizes homosexual conduct.

1998 – Cyprus decriminalizes homosexual conduct.

1998 – South African Constitutional Court rules sodomy not a crime.

2006 – Hong Kong removes discriminatory age of consent for sex between men.

2010 – Homosexual conduct made legal in Fiji under the *Crimes Decree 2010*.

2014 – The Turkish Republic of Northern Cyprus decriminalizes homosexual conduct.

2016 – Nauru Crimes Act of 2016 repeals penal code (based on QCC), decriminalizing homosexual conduct.

Belize's Supreme Court declared Belize's anti-sodomy law unconstitutional.

Seychelles government decriminalizes homosexual conduct

Notes

1 Elizabeth Kolsky, "Codification and the Rule of Colonial Difference: Criminal Procedure in British India," *Law and History Review* 23, no. 3 (2005): 631–2.
2 HC Deb 10 July 1833, vol. 19, c533.
3 Sanford H. Kadish, "Codifiers of the Criminal Law: Wechsler's Predecessors," *Columbia Law Review* 78, no. 5 (1978): 1110.
4 David Skuy, "Macaulay and the Indian Penal Code of 1862: The Myth of the Inherent Superiority and Modernity of the English Legal System Compared to India's Legal System in the Nineteenth Century," *Modern Asian Studies* 32 (1998): 518.
5 Ibid., 539–40.
6 Thomas Babington Macaulay, Baron Macaulay, *The Indian Penal Code, as Originally Framed in 1837* (Madras: Higginbotham, 1888), 64.
7 Ibid., 156.
8 Alok Gupta, *This Alien Legacy: The Origins of "Sodomy" Laws in British Colonialism* (New York: Human Rights Watch, 2008), 18.
9 Aengus Carroll and Lucas Ramon Mendos, "State-Sponsored Homophobia," *ILGA* (2017), 133.
10 Lynette J. Chua Kher Shing, "Saying No: Sections 377 and 377A of the Penal Code," *Singapore Journal of Legal Studies* (2003): 215.
11 Nang Yin Kham, "An Introduction to the Law and Judicial System of Myanmar," *CALS Working Paper Series 14/2* (March 2014), 2; Macaulay, *The Indian Penal Code, as Originally Framed in 1837*, 156.
12 Sinha Basnayake, "The Anglo-Indian Codes in Ceylon," *International and Comparative Law Quarterly* 22, no. 2 (1973): 286.
13 Carroll and Mendos, "State-Sponsored Homophobia," 137.
14 Sumit Baudh, "Decriminalisation of Consensual Same-Sex Sexual Acts in the South Asian Commonwealth: Struggles in Contexts," in *Human Rights, Sexual Orientation and Gender Identity in the Commonwealth: Struggles for Decriminalisation and Change* (London: Institute of Commonwealth Studies, School of Advanced Study, University of London, 2013), 287–311.
15 Michael Kirby, "Discrimination on the Ground of Sexual Orientation: A New Initiative for the Commonwealth of Nations?," *The Commonwealth Lawyer* (May 2007), 24.
16 Gupta, *This Alien Legacy*, 6.
17 Michael Bohlander, "Criminalising LGBT Persons Under National Criminal Law and Article 7(1)(h) and (3) of the ICC Statute," *Global Policy* 5, no. 4 (2014): 401–14.
18 Husnu Al Suood, *The Maldivian Legal System* (Male: Maldives Law Institute, 2014), 86.
19 Obtained from the International Labor Organization's NatLex, which sourced it from the Maldives Attorney General's Office website, www.ilo.org/dyn/natlex/natlex4.detail?p_lang=&p_isn=85770&p_classification=01.04.
20 Gupta, *This Alien Legacy*, 21–2.
21 Olaf Köndgen, *The Codification of Islamic Criminal Law in the Sudan: Penal Codes and Supreme Court Case Law Under Numayrī and Al-Bashīr* (Leiden: Brill, 2017), 185–6.
22 Ibid., 186–7.
23 Carroll and Mendos, "State-Sponsored Homophobia," 100.

24 Martin L. Friedland, "R. S. Wright's Model Criminal Code: A Forgotten Chapter in the History of the Criminal Law," *Oxford Journal of Legal Studies* 1, no. 3 (1981): 313.
25 Ibid., 328.
26 Robert S. Wright, *Drafts of a Criminal Code and a Code of Criminal Procedure for the Island of Jamaica With an Explanatory Memorandum* (London: Great Britain Parliament, 1877).
27 Ibid., 117.
28 "Consolidated Laws of the Colony of British Honduras, 1887," London: Waterlow and Sons.
29 "About Orozco v AG," Faculty of Law University of West Indies Rights Advocacy Project (U-RAP), www.u-rap.org/web2/index.php/2015-09-29-00-40-03/orozco-v-attorney-general-of-belize/item/2-caleb-orozco-v-attorney-general-of-belize-and-others.
30 Friedland, "R. S. Wright's Model Criminal Code," 337.
31 James S. Read, "Ghana: The Criminal Code, 1960," *International and Comparative Law Quarterly* 11, no. 1 (1962): 272.
32 Records of Ghana Criminal Code 1960 can be accessed at www.wipo.int/edocs/lexdocs/laws/en/gh/gh010en.pdf.
33 Friedland, "R. S. Wright's Model Criminal Code," 316.
34 Martin L. Friedland, "Codification in the Commonwealth: Earlier Efforts," *Commonwealth Law Bulletin* 18, no. 3 (1992): 1176.
35 Ibid.
36 Records of the "Bill to Establish a Code of Offences for England and Ireland, and to Prescribe the Procedure by Indictment for the Punishment of Offenders, 1880" can be accessed at http://ozcase.library.qut.edu.au/qhlc/documents/CrimCode_Bill_1880.pdf.
37 The Queensland code became the basis of a wide variety of criminal codes across the world and is discussed in more detail later in the chapter.
38 Barry Wright, "Criminal Law Codification and Imperial Projects: The Self-Governing Jurisdiction Codes of the 1890's," *Legal History* 12, no. 1 (2008): 34.
39 Desmond H. Brown, ed., *The Birth of a Criminal Code: The Evolution of Canada's Justice System* (Toronto: University of Toronto Press, 1995), 261–4.
40 Records of the "1892 Canada Criminal Code" can be accessed at https://archive.org/details/criminalcodevic00canagoog.
41 Wright, "Criminal Law Codification and Imperial Projects," 38.
42 Records of the "New Zealand Criminal Code Act 1893" can be accessed at www.nzlii.org/nz/legis/hist_act/cca189357v1893n56192/ Accessed 12/14/2017.
43 Geraldine Mackenzie, "An Enduring Influence: Sir Samuel Griffith and His Contribution to Criminal Justice in Queensland," *Queensland University of Technology Law & Justice Journal* 2, no. 1 (2002): 59.
44 Records of the "Criminal Code Act 1899" can be found through Ozcase Queensland Historical Legal Collection at http://ozcase.library.qut.edu.au/qhlc/documents/CrimCode1899_63Vic_9.pdf.
45 Robin S. O'Regan, *New Essays on the Australian Criminal Codes* (Sydney: Law Book Company, 1988), 104.
46 Records of "Criminal Code Act 1902 of Western Australia" can be accessed at www.slp.wa.gov.au/legislation/statutes.nsf/law_a6302.html.
47 O'Regan, *New Essays on the Australian Criminal Codes*, 118.

48 Melissa Bull, Susan Pinto, and Paul Wilson, *Homosexual Law Reform in Australia* (Canberra: Australian Institute of Criminology, 1991), 2.
49 O'Regan, *New Essays on the Australian Criminal Codes*, 105.
50 Carroll and Mendos, "State-Sponsored Homophobia," 142.
51 Harry Gibbs, "Queensland Criminal Code: From Italy to Zanzibar," *Australian Law Journal* 77, no. 4 (2003): 237.
52 Carroll and Mendos, "State-Sponsored Homophobia," 36.
53 Robin S. O'Regan, "Sir Samuel Griffith's Criminal Code," *Journal of the Royal Historical Society of Queensland* 14, no. 8 (1991): 313.
54 Kenneth Brown, "Criminal Law and Custom in Solomon Islands," *Queensland University of Technology Law Journal* 2 (1986): 134–5.
55 O'Regan, *New Essays on the Australian Criminal Codes*, 113.
56 Records of the "Bermuda Criminal Code Amendment Act 1994" can be accessed at www.bermudalaws.bm/Laws/Annual%20Laws/1994/Acts/Criminal%20Code%20Amendment%20Act%201994.pdf.
57 Henry Francis Morris, "How Nigeria Got Its Criminal Code," *Journal of African Law* 14, no. 3 (1970): 139.
58 Ibid., 144.
59 Henry Francis Morris and James S. Read, *Indirect Rule and the Search for Justice: Essays in East African Legal History* (Oxford: Oxford University Press, 1972), 113–15.
60 Henry Francis Morris, "A History of the Adoption of Codes of Criminal Law and Procedure in British Colonial Africa, 1876–1935," *Journal of African Law* 18, no. 1 (1974): 15.
61 Barry Wright, "Self-Governing Codifications of English Criminal Law and Empire: The Queensland and Canadian Examples," *University of Queensland Law Journal* 26, no. 1 (2007): 39–65.
62 Morris and Read, *Indirect Rule and the Search for Justice*, 122–4.
63 Morris, "A History of the Adoption of Codes of Criminal Law and Procedure in British Colonial Africa, 1876–1935," 17–22.
64 I. G. Brewer, "Sources of the Criminal Law of Botswana," *Journal of African Law* 18, no. 1 (1974): 25–6.
65 Ibid., 28.
66 Records of the "Botswana Penal Code Law No. 2 of 1964" can be accessed at www.wipo.int/edocs/lexdocs/laws/en/bw/bw012en.pdf.
67 Scott Long, "Before the Law: Criminalizing Sexual Conduct in Colonial and Post-colonial Southern African Societies," in *More than a Name: State-Sponsored Homophobia and Its Consequences in Southern Africa*, ed. Human Rights Watch & The International Gay and Lesbian Human Rights Commission (New York: Human Rights Watch, 2009).
68 Records of the "Baghdad Penal Code 1919" can be accessed at http://gjpi.org/wp-content/uploads/baghdad-penal-code-of-1919.pdf.
69 Arno Schmitt and Jehoeda Sofer, *Sexuality and Eroticism Among Males in Moslem Societies* (Binghamton, NY: Routledge, 1992), 137.
70 Records of the "Iraq 1969 Penal Code" can be accessed at www.refworld.org/cgi-bin/texis/vtx/rwmain?page=country&docid=452524304&skip=0&category=LEGAL&coi=IRQ&querysi=penal%20code&searchin=title&sort=date.
71 See http://gjpi.org/2009/05/21/homosexuality-and-the-criminal-law-in-iraq/.
72 Schmitt and Sofer, *Sexuality and Eroticism Among Males in Moslem Societies*, 133.

73 Herbert J. Liebesny, "Administration and Legal Development in Arabia: The Persian Gulf Principalities," *Middle East Journal* 10, no. 1 (1956): 37.
74 Nathan J. Brown, *The Rule of Law in the Arab World: Courts in Egypt and the Gulf* (Cambridge; New York: Cambridge University Press, 1997), 142.
75 Ibid., 143.
76 Ibid., 147.
77 Carroll and Mendos, "State-Sponsored Homophobia," 30.
78 O'Regan, "Sir Samuel Griffith's Criminal Code," 314.
79 Orna Alyagon Darr, "Narratives of 'Sodomy' and 'Unnatural Offenses' in the Courts of Mandate Palestine (1918–48)," *Law and History Review* 35, no. 1 (2017): 244. https://doi.org/10.1017/S0738248016000493.
80 Norman Abrams, "Interpreting the Criminal Code Ordinance, 1935 – The Untapped Well," *Israel Law Review* 7, no. 1 (1972): 29.
81 O'Regan, *New Essays on the Australian Criminal Codes*, 112.
82 This can be accessed at www.track.unodc.org/LegalLibrary/LegalResources/Israel/Laws/Israel%20Penal%20Code%201977.pdf.
83 Long, "Before the Law: Criminalizing Sexual Conduct in Colonial and Post-colonial Southern African Societies."
84 Ibid.
85 Carroll and Mendos, "State-Sponsored Homophobia," 106.
86 Sydney Malupande, *Human Rights in Zambia: Freedom of Sexual Orientation, Homosexual Law Reform* (University of Zambia, 2000), http://dspace.unza.zm:8080/xmlui/bitstream/handle/123456789/2952/MALUPANDE0001.PDF?sequence=1&isAllowed=y
87 Carroll and Mendos, "State-Sponsored Homophobia," 105.
88 Records of Swaziland's 1939 "Criminal Law and Procedure Act" can be accessed at www.unodc.org/res/cld/document/swz/1938/criminal_procedure_and_evidence_act_html/Swaziland_Criminal_Procedure_and_Evidence_Act_1938.pdf. Accessed 12/17/2017.
89 Carroll and Mendos, "State-Sponsored Homophobia," 100.
90 William McClain, "Criminal Law Treatment of Sexual Activity," *University of Lesotho Faculty of Social Sciences Staff Seminar Paper No. 19* (1979), 28.
91 A. J. Kerr, "The Reception and Codification of Systems of Law in Southern Africa," *Journal of African Law* 2, no. 2 (1958): 89.
92 Carroll and Mendos, "State-Sponsored Homophobia," 27.
93 Records of the "Offences Against the Person Act, 1861" can be accessed at www.legislation.gov.uk/ukpga/Vict/24-25/100/section/61/enacted. Accessed 1/07/2017.
94 Carroll and Mendos, "State-Sponsored Homophobia," 114.
95 Joseph Gaskins Jr., "'Buggery' and the Commonwealth Caribbean: A Comparative Examination of the Bahamas, Jamaica, and Trinidad and Tobago," in *Human Rights, Sexual Orientation and Gender Identity in the Commonwealth: Struggles for Decriminalisation and Change* (London: Institute of Commonwealth Studies, School of Advanced Study, University of London, 2013), 431.
96 Carroll and Mendos, "State-Sponsored Homophobia," 143.
97 Richard W. Whitecross, "The Thrimzhung Chenmo and the Emergence of the Contemporary Bhutanese Legal System," in *The Spider and the Piglet: Collected Papers on Bhutanese Society*, ed. Karma Ura and Sonam Kinga (Thimphu: Center for Bhutan Studies, 2004).
98 Records of the "Bhutan Penal Code" can be accessed at http://oag.gov.bt/wp-content/uploads/2010/05/Penal-Code-of-Bhutan-2004_English-version_.pdf.

99 David John Frank, Steven A. Boutcher, and Bayliss Camp, "The Reform of Sodomy Laws: From a World Society Perspective," in *Queer Mobilizations: LGBT Activists Confront the Law*, ed. S. Barclay, M. Berstein, and A. M. Marshall (New York: New York University Press, 2009), 533.
100 Carroll and Mendos, "State-Sponsored Homophobia," 128.
101 Note that section 318 only criminalizes "carnal intercourse against the order of nature with any person without his consent."

3 Empirical analysis of colonial legacies around the world

Are modern states more likely to currently criminalize homosexuality if they were a British colony than if they were not? Also, are former British colonies less likely or slower to decriminalize on average than the former colonies of other European imperialists? In this chapter, we investigate these two claims using systematic data analysis. We use a dataset that includes data on 185 countries to assess the overall evidentiary basis for the preceding two claims. We find that British colonies are much more likely to have laws that criminalize homosexual conduct than other colonies or other states in general. This result holds after controlling for numerous variables that might be expected to influence the likelihood of repressive LGBT rights legislation. However, we also find that the evidence in favor of the claim that British imperialism "poisoned" societies against homosexuality is inconclusive at best. The speed of decriminalization of homosexual conduct for those colonies with such a law is not systematically slower for British colonies compared to colonies of other European states. This suggests that the stickiness of repressive institutions is relatively constant and not a product of a particular type of colonialism.

Although many countries have decriminalized, homosexual conduct still remains a crime in 72 countries in the world by 2018, according to the ILGA.[1] Most of these laws target male to male sexual relationships, while only a few countries also criminalize female to female relationships. According to the information provided by ILGA, there are different types of punishment for homosexual conduct: fines or restrictions or penal labor, imprisonment, and the death penalty. As we can see from Table 3.1, most countries in this group consider homosexual conduct punishable by imprisonment. Only in eight countries is homosexual conduct considered severe enough for punishment by death penalty. For example, the Islamic penal code of Iran of 1991 states "sodomy involves killing if both the active and passive persons are mature, of sound mind and have free will."[2]

Table 3.1 Countries where homosexuality is criminalized (2018)

Fines or restrictions or penal labor	*Imprisonment of less than ten years*	*Imprisonment of ten years or more*	*Death penalty*
Angola	Afghanistan	Bangladesh	Iran
	Algeria	Barbados	Mauritania
	Antigua and Barbuda	Dominica	Nigeria
	Bhutan	Ethiopia	Qatar
	Botswana	Gambia	Saudi Arabia
	Brunei Darussalam	Grenada	Somalia
	Burundi	Guyana	Sudan
	Cameroon	India	Yemen, Rep.
	Comoros	Kenya	
	Egypt, Arab Rep.	Kiribati	
	Eritrea	Libya	
	Ghana	Malawi	
	Guinea	Malaysia	
	Indonesia	Papua New Guinea	
	Jamaica	Sierra Leone	
	Kuwait	St. Lucia	
	Lebanon	St. Vincent and the Grenadines	
	Liberia	Swaziland	
	Maldives	Tanzania	
	Mauritius	Tonga	
	Morocco	Trinidad and Tobago	
	Myanmar	Tuvalu	
	Oman	Uganda	
	Pakistan	United Arab Emirates	
	Samoa	West Bank and Gaza	
	Senegal	Zambia	
	Singapore		
	Solomon Islands		
	South Sudan		
	Sri Lanka		
	St. Kitts and Nevis		
	Syrian Arab Republic		
	Togo		
	Tunisia		
	Turkmenistan		
	Uzbekistan		
	Zimbabwe		

Existing literature

The first claim, which has recently attained popularity, is the idea that the British Empire was responsible for spreading laws that criminalized homosexual conduct amongst its colonies, whereas other imperialists did not.[3] The second claim is that there is some legacy of the British colonial experience that has made it less likely for countries that are former British colonies to decriminalize homosexual conduct. The claim is that not only did the British bring such laws to their colonies, but that they "poisoned" the prospects for liberalization and the repeal of those laws. Tielman and Hammelburg argue that

> From a historical perspective, the English legislation against homosexuality has had (and unfortunately still has) appalling consequences for the legal position of homosexual men, and, to a lesser extent, lesbians in the former British colonies. The effects of the former French, Dutch, Spanish, and Portuguese colonial legislation against homosexuality are less severe.[4]

Wilets also claims that the effects of colonialism even after independence are such that Caribbean nations, mostly former British colonies, have "extraordinarily high levels of anti-LGBT social animosity and repressive legislation" whereas Latin American nations, mostly former Spanish colonies, do not.[5] This argument is essentially that British colonialism not only spread such laws, but also created long-term barriers to decriminalization.

Research questions and hypotheses

Are former British colonies more likely to have laws that criminalize homosexual conduct? The first research question can be answered by looking at the current state of LGBT rights legislation around the world. Existing studies have not used statistical techniques to control for other factors that are potentially correlated with levels of LGBT tolerance or repression. We use data on a variety of variables to provide evidence relevant to the following hypothesis:

> *H1: States with a British legal origin are more likely to have a law criminalizing homosexual conduct.*

Our second research question concerns the legacy of colonialism post-independence. Do British colonies have a harder time decriminalizing homosexual conduct laws once they are free of the "imperialist yoke"? This is a complex question, but there are simple ways of using the existing data to provide suggestive conclusions. If it is harder for a state to decriminalize homosexual conduct, then it should take longer, ceteris paribus, for such a state to do so. Therefore, if British colonialism has entrenched homophobia deeper than other colonies, it should have taken longer for British colonies to decriminalize than other states, or colonies of other imperialists. One way of operationalizing this idea is to look at the length of time between a colony gaining independence and decriminalization of homosexual conduct.

This leads to the following hypothesis:

> *H2: States with a British legal origin have a longer time in between gaining their independence and decriminalizing homosexual conduct.*

However, since the 1960s there has been a global trend toward decriminalization of homosexual conduct. Frank, Boutcher, and Camp explicitly address the issue of the worldwide trend towards the decriminalization of sodomy.[6] Based on a dataset of legal changes since 1945, including expansions and contractions in the scope of the criminal regulation of sodomy, they argue that domestic-level factors are insufficient to explain the liberalization of sodomy regulation on a global scale in a short period of time. Instead, they turn to a world society perspective and claim that the world culture is becoming more tolerant of homosexuality in general. This argument rightfully noticed the global trend towards decriminalization of homosexual conduct, however by itself it is unable to account for variation in the continuation of criminalization of homosexual conduct among various countries in the world to this day. That means a world society type of argument cannot easily explain why certain countries still maintain such laws. This is especially true for variation associated with colonial heritage. There is no reason why former British colonies would be less open to the influences of global culture. In fact, given their relatively high level of economic development and civil liberties, they are probably more receptive to global society than other countries that have less access. However, if there is a global move towards acceptance of homosexuality, then merely looking at the time between independence and decriminalization risks omitting a crucial variable if colonies gained independence at different points in world time, which they did. In order to deal with this issue, we also look at whether British colonies have decriminalized homosexual conduct later in world time than others. This motivates an alternative operationalization of the concept of time to decriminalization, providing the following hypothesis.

> *H3: States with a British legal origin take longer to decriminalize after 1945.*

We chose 1945 because we wanted to focus on the modern era; and it seems reasonable to argue that the post–World War II time represents a clear juncture in world history during which some fundamental changes occurred in the international system. If H2 or H3 are not borne out in the data, then this is evidence against the idea that British colonialism uniquely created barriers to the decriminalization of homosexual conduct. If indeed H2 or H3, or both, are supported by our empirical analysis, then we can be more confident in stating that British colonialism created political and social legacies that have made repeal of those laws more difficult.

Data and methodology

Data for our analysis come from several sources. The dependent variable – criminalization of homosexual conduct – comes from the ILGA's website. We coded this dependent variable in two ways. First, we constructed a dummy variable – 1 indicating criminalization of homosexual conduct is present and 0 otherwise. We also constructed an ordinal variable following the coding scheme provided by the ILGA's website – that is 4 for death penalty, 3 for imprisonment of more than ten years, 2 for imprisonment of less than ten years, 1 for fines or restrictions or penal labor, and 0 for none. All the coding here follows strictly ILGA's own coding, and we cut off the time by the end of summer 2010.

Given the central importance of the colonialism variable, we used several different measures. Initially, we used the legal system origin data compiled by La Porta et al.[7] This data is widely considered to be the most systematically collected data on the colonial origins of legal systems. Given that our research concerns the legal status of LGBT rights, this seemed to be an appropriate measure. However, we also used other measures of colonial experience, in order to see if the results were sensitive to this particular coding. The coding for the other colonialism variables was taken from a variety of sources. One was Bernhard, Reenock, and Nordstrom, who had coded British, French, Spanish, Dutch, Portuguese, and US colonial possessions.[8] Lange, Mahoney, and vom Hau[9] coded British and Spanish colonies only, and Klerman et al.[10] coded British and French colonies as well as countries not colonized by the French but that had adopted French civil law codes. The variable for whether a state had been a colony was the union of the sets of overseas western colonies identified in our three main sources.[11] This categorization excludes Soviet, German, US, and Belgian colonies. Soviet Socialist Republics were not colonized or decolonized in the same way as other colonies and their inclusion would bias the results. There were not enough German, American, or Belgian colonies to draw meaningful statistical results. The key variable of whether a state was a British colony was the union of the sets of British colonies identified by Bernhard et al., Lange et al., and Klerman et al. We used Klerman et al.'s coding of French colonies, as they had the most comprehensive list.

For the specific dates of decriminalization of homosexual conduct, we aggregated data from several sources. The data came from Waaldijk (2009); Bruce-Jones and Itaborahy (2011); and Frank, Camp, and Boutcher (2010).[12] Differences between codings in these sources were almost entirely in terms of coverage, rather than different dates. Where these sources conflicted, we applied a majority rule; that is, one source was overruled by two sources.

For the question of whether some states took longer between independence and decriminalization than other states, we needed to know when states became independent. The coding for the start date of states was taken from the Polity dataset and supplemented by the authors' own coding for those states not covered by the Polity dataset.

In addition, our dataset includes a set of control variables. One commonly posited theory about social tolerance and attitudes towards homosexuality is modernization.[13] Therefore, one might expect a positive relationship between economic development and tolerant policies towards homosexual conduct. Other studies have also shown attitudes towards homosexuality are highly correlated with economic inequality in a given country.[14] Thus, we also control for countries' economic inequality using the Gini index. Religion is also commonly considered to be an important factor in the legal treatment of LGBT people.[15] There are two ways religion can manifest in policies towards homosexuality: one is the overall level of religiosity of a given country, and the other is that country's dominant religious denomination. The measurement of religiosity comes from the World Values Survey, which is an eight-category index of religious institution attendance. To measure religious denominations for countries, we used the Fractionalization data compiled by Alesina et al. (2003).[16] Furthermore, we can also think that a country's regime type may also matter as to whether laws that criminalize homosexual conduct exist in its law books. Democracies are probably less likely to persecute homosexuality than authoritarian ones, presumably due to democratic countries' tolerance towards minorities, their emphasis on equal rights, and their tendency to protect fundamental human rights.[17] To measure the level of democracy and authoritarianism for each country in our dataset, we used the Polity dataset.

We also believe a set of international variables need to be controlled. As the world is increasingly interconnected, the social aspect of globalization means more intensive transmission of ideas and information from the outside world. Thus, we can expect that countries that are most open to the outside world – embodying 'cosmopolitan culture' as phrased by Norris and Inglehart – are most likely to decriminalize homosexual conduct.[18]

To measure countries' openness to cosmopolitan values, we used Internet usage as a proxy, for which we used the number of Internet users per 100 people. Data for Internet usage is from the World Bank Development Index. Finally, international human rights regime might also play role here. The continuation of laws that criminalize homosexual conduct in many countries has become a target of international human rights campaign. For example, Amnesty International, Human Rights Watch, and many others have devoted campaigns for the decriminalization of homosexual conduct, and have called for the release of anyone imprisoned solely for homosexuality as prisoners of conscience.[19] Therefore, we believe countries that are most open to international human rights norms are the ones most likely to decriminalize homosexual conduct. To measure the influence of the international human rights regime, we used the number of major human rights, humanitarian, disarmament, and environmental treaties ratified by countries, which we sourced from *Global Civil Society*.[20]

Our main model for the current legal status of homosexual conduct uses a dummy variable for whether there is a criminalization of homosexual conduct and we estimate the coefficients of the independent variables using logistic regression with robust standard errors. As our data on religiosity is limited to less than half of the cases, we estimate the model separately after controlling for religiosity. We also use an ordinal dependent variable, which includes the severity of legal punishment, and estimate the models using ordinal logit. For the models using time to decriminalization, an interval variable, as the dependent variable, we estimated linear regression models with robust standard errors. For a list of descriptive statistics of our variables, see Table 3.2. Results for our first set of models addressing H1 (concerning the contemporary distribution of laws that criminalize homosexual conduct) are reported in Table 3.3.

Table 3.2 Summary statistics

Variable	*Mean*	*Std. Dev.*	*Min.*	*Max.*	*N*
Shii Muslim	2.248	11.167	0	93.89	185
Sunni Muslim	20.708	33.656	0	99.89	185
Protestant	16.169	23.409	0	89.29	185
Catholic	29.127	34.424	0	96.01	185
Human Rights Treaties	17.795	3.859	7	22	166
Inequality (Gini)	40.557	8.745	24.7	64.3	134
Democracy (Polity)	3.733	6.396	−10	10	150
Religiosity	4.649	1.37	2.29	7.63	89
Per Capita GDP (ppp)	13245	14954	314	88775	163
British Legal Origin	0.315	0.466	0	1	178

Table 3.3 Tests of colonial rule on laws criminalizing homosexual conduct

	Bivariate	*Colony Dummies*	*With Religiosity*	*Full*	*With Religiosity*
British	2.388***	2.505***	2.414***	4.381***	6.223
	(0.408)	(0.422)	(0.741)	(1.505)	(4.195)
French		0.560	1.539	–1.125	1.280
		(0.470)	(1.269)	(0.850)	(1.632)
Religiosity			0.793***		0.541
			(0.219)		(0.598)
Shii Muslim				0.0175	0.0313
				(0.0190)	(0.0203)
Sunni Muslim				0.0363***	0.0403*
				(0.0104)	(0.0214)
Catholic				0.0728	0.0226
				(0.0152)	(0.0300)
Protestant				0.00760	0.0525
				(0.0280)	(0.0423)
Internet				–0.0453	–0.119
				(0.0338)	(0.0874)
Per Capita GDP (ppp)				–0.451	0.355
				(0.484)	(0.806)
Inequality (Gini)				0.00416	–0.227
				(0.0569)	(0.182)
Democracy (Polity)				–0.147**	–0.322**
				(0.0660)	(0.129)
HR Treaties				–0.191	–0.426
				(0.119)	(0.309)
Constant	–1.079***	–1.196***	–6.554***	5.538	7.733
	(0.196)	(0.224)	(1.213)	(5.494)	(14.99)
Observations	185	185	89	126	79

Standard errors in parentheses. *$p < .10$, **$p < 0.05$, ***$p < 0.01$

The prevalence of laws that criminalize homosexual conduct and British legal origin

One of the major findings of our data analysis is the correlation between having a British legal origin and having a law criminalizing homosexual conduct. Of those states with such a law, 57 percent of them have a British legal origin. Of those states with a British legal origin, almost 70 percent of them continue to criminalize homosexual conduct. We estimated the coefficient on British legal origin in this bivariate situation using logit with robust standard errors. Those states with a British legal origin are significantly more likely to have such a law. In fact, the predicted probability change (as British legal origin goes from 0 to 1) is from 0.24 to 0.7, an increase of 46 percentage points. This relationship remains statistically significant and substantively large across numerous model specifications. Even after controlling for measures of religion, modernity, wealth, inequality, democracy, and human rights treaties signed, the effect size is large (see results in Table 3.3). In Model 1 with a criminalization dummy dependent variable, the increase in the predicted probability of such a law is from 0.04 to almost 0.80, while other variables are held at their means. This increase of 75 percentage points dwarfs all other effect sizes in this model. After controlling for religiosity, using the smaller sample of 81, the effect size is larger and is still significant at the 5 percent level ($p = 0.048$). In a model including only British legal origin and religiosity as independent variables, British legal origin is highly significant ($p = 0.002$). When using the ordinal punishment measure as the dependent variable and estimating effects using ordinal logit, the effect size is similarly large and significant, again even after controlling for religiosity.

What are the possible explanations for the large difference in the probability of having a law that criminalizes homosexual conduct between those states with and without a British legal origin? Given the data at hand, the relationship looks robust and strong. Why might this be the case? A selection effect seems unlikely; this would require that Britain colonized countries with some sort of predisposition to homophobia. The most plausible story involves a contingent and path dependent process of institutional evolution. This type of process is a prominent one in the discussion of colonial and postcolonial development.[21] The most obvious pathway is that at the time when British colonies developed their legal systems, homosexuality was illegal in the United Kingdom and this law was transplanted into colonial law. Homosexuality was not legalized in England and Wales until 1967, after many colonies became independent and so any changes in British law were not similarly transferred into the colonial context. Absent a strong domestic constituency in favor of repeal of homophobic legislation, these laws remain on the books in former British colonies across the world.

What about other colonial legal origins? Table 3.4 shows the distribution of decriminalization status by colonial status. The other wide-ranging global

Table 3.4 Decriminalization status by colonial status

	British Colony	*French Colony*	*Spanish Colony*	*Other*
Never criminalized	–	10	–	2
Decriminalized before independence	–	3	1	13
Decriminalized after independence	11	1	16	44
Not yet decriminalized	36	9	–	31

NB: Cell counts are frequencies. Total = 177

empire, the French, did not spread laws against sodomy or homosexuality because the Revolutionary Constituent Assembly of 1789–91 abrogated the previous law against sodomy in France when they adopted the French penal code of 1791.[22] In a bivariate situation the coefficient on French legal origin is both negative and insignificant. After controlling for British legal origin, it becomes positive and significant ($p = 0.017$) and its marginal effect on predicted probability is 35 percentage points. However, after controlling for the other independent variables it decreases in significance ($p = 0.164$) and becomes negative in terms of substantive effect. This relationship is thus not as robust as the one between British legal origin and criminalization of homosexual conduct laws.

One consequence of the large effect size of the British legal origin variable might be that the predicted probability of other independent variables varies according to whether they have a British legal origin. That is, the effect of another variable, say democracy, might be different for states whose laws have British legal origin compared to other states. Two other relatively significant variables in the full model are the number of Sunni Muslims in the country and the countries' polity score. The effects of increased democracy are more pronounced for countries of British legal origin when the polity score goes from 0 to 10 than when it goes from –10 to 0. That is, there is an increasing marginal effect of democracy for states that have laws with British legal origin. The opposite is true of states of other legal origins; there is a decreasing marginal effect of democracy for these states. However, this is not true for the effect of percentage of Sunni Muslims in a state. The marginal effect of an increasing percentage of Sunnis is declining for those with British legal origin and increasing for those without. In both of these situations, there are substantial differences between such states and others.

Robustness tests

It is possible that there could be an objection to our use of the La Porta et al.'s measure of legal origin.[23] This measure does not directly operationalize colonial heritage, and some of the states coded as having a British legal origin do not obviously fit the pattern of overseas formal imperialism. As a means of testing the sensitivity of the results to the particular coding of the legal origin variable, we used colonialism data from a variety of alternative sources. One prominent analysis from political science of the legacy of colonialism is Bernhard, Reenock, and Nordstrom.[24] They investigated the correlation between the longevity of democratic political systems and experience of colonialism. They found that, compared to countries with other western overseas colonial legacies, British colonies have experienced longer periods of democracy. "The British colonial legacy is quite conducive to survival [of democracy] compared with the others."[25] Using their coding for European Overseas Colonialism, excluding settler colonies and internal European colonies, the results are similar to those obtained using La Porta et al.'s data.

Compared to other colonies, British colonies are overwhelmingly more likely to have laws that criminalize homosexual conduct. None of the French or Spanish colonies identified by Bernhard, Reenock, and Nordstrom currently have such laws. Of a total of 30 former colonies with such laws, 27 are former British colonies, and all but three former British colonies have such laws. Of the other colonies with such laws, two are Portuguese and one is Dutch. Compared to all 155 other countries, former British colonies are 22 times more likely to have laws that criminalize homosexual conduct.

We estimated the full model using four additional measures of British colonial origin. Each of the codings of British colonial status from Bernhard et al., Lange et al., and Klerman et al., as well as the aggregate measure of the union of all of these, produce coefficients that are similar in size and statistical significance to La Porta et al.'s British legal origin data.

Effect of colonial legacy on time to decriminalization

The second question, apart from whether and how much British colonies are more likely to have criminalization of homosexual conduct laws, is whether different colonial legacies had different effects in terms of the likelihood of decriminalization post-decolonization. That is, did British colonialism affect the long-term trajectory of LGBT rights in their colonies? Or has the imposition of such laws been easily shrugged off as soon as colonies became free to control their own destiny? In this section, we analyze the data to provide some evidence relevant to this question. One crucial fact to establish is whether it takes longer to decriminalize homosexual conduct after decolonization for British colonies. Another question is whether former British colonies are taking longer to decriminalize relative to the general global trend towards decriminalization. In order to answer these questions, we generated two operationalizations of the concept of time to decriminalization; one based on the time colonies took to decriminalize after they gained their independence from the colonial state, and one based on the time all states took to decriminalize after World War II.

The overall trend globally has been towards decriminalization. The differences by colonial identity are striking. Figures 3.1 and 3.2, and Tables 3.4 and 3.5 show that the trends of decriminalization are different for French, Spanish, and British colonies.

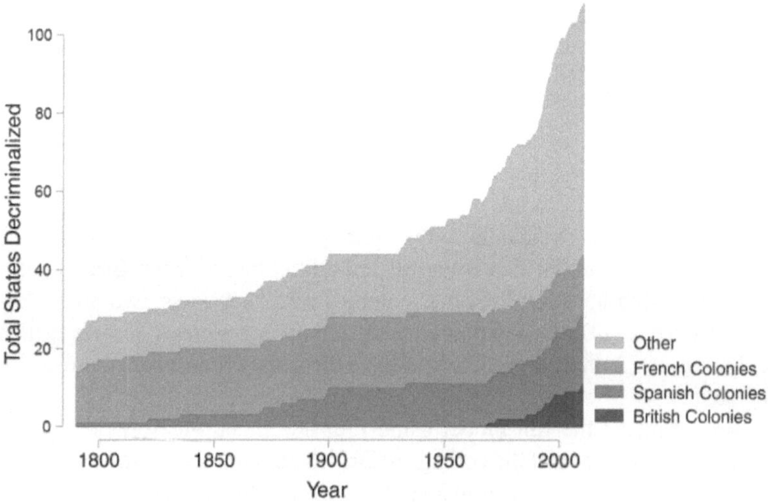

Figure 3.1 The decriminalization of homosexual conduct

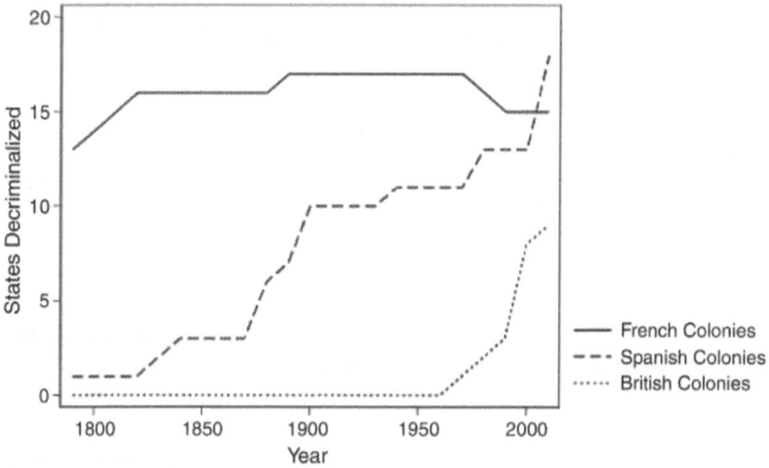

Figure 3.2 The decriminalization of homosexual conduct

First, we compared the time to decriminalization from decolonization for states that had been colonized by Britain, France, or Spain. The aim here is to see whether there has been some sort of specific legacy of British colonialism that has increased the time between becoming independent and

Table 3.5 Time to decriminalization by colonial heritage

	British	*French*	*Spanish*	*Other*
Independence to decriminalization	75	29	94	76
1945 to decriminalization	48	–	47	38
Independence to 2010 / not yet decriminalized	45	49	–	64

Note: Cell counts are mean years. Recriminalizations excluded.

decriminalization. We excluded from the analysis those colonies in which there is no evidence that there has ever been such a law, those colonies that decriminalized prior to independence, and those that have not yet decriminalized, which leaves us with 72 states. Then we defined a variable representing the time it took after a colony gained its independence for it to decriminalize homosexual conduct.

Time to decriminalization after independence
= Year of decriminalization – Year of independence[26]

The mean time to decriminalization for British colonies was about 75 years. For French colonies, it was 29 years. However, the mean time to decriminalization for Spanish colonies was 94 years, and for states that have another colonial heritage, the average time to decriminalization from independence is 76 years. British colonies thus do not appear at this level to be different from other types of states.

Next, we compared the time to decriminalization after World War II for states that had a criminalization of homosexual conduct law in the year 1945. This eliminated states that did not criminalize homosexual conduct in the year 1945, as well as states that have not yet decriminalized (as of 2010). This left 60 states. No French colonies decriminalized during this time (although three recriminalized; discussed later in the chapter). Then we defined a variable representing the time it took for a state to decriminalize after 1945. This was defined as:

Time to decriminalization = Year of decriminalization – 1945

The mean time to decriminalization for British colonies is 48 years. The mean time to decriminalization for colonies of Spanish colonies was 47 years. There is no appreciable difference between these two mean times to decriminalization.

It is true that there are more British colonies yet to decriminalize than any other category and almost as many states that have not yet decriminalized are British colonies than not. By itself, however, this does not yet mean that we have evidence that the British colonial experience has uniquely delayed decriminalization. If we define a third variable, the time from independence to the present (2010), for those states that have not yet decriminalized we can see that less time has passed from independence to decriminalization for British colonies than for French or for other states. This third variable will, of course, change in the future, but as of yet the evidence does not favor the idea that British colonies have a harder time decriminalizing than other types of states.

By 2008 no former Spanish colonies had laws that criminalize homosexual conduct. The distribution of decriminalization dates is instructive (see Figure 3.2). Of 18, ten had decriminalized by 1900. Then, between 1900 and 1971 only Uruguay decriminalized. There were thus two waves in which former Spanish colonies got rid of such laws; one from 1871 to 1900 and one from 1971 to 2008. This complicates the issue of mean time to decriminalization. For the first wave, the mean time to decriminalization from independence was 44 years. For the second wave, it was 136 years. It is not convincing that Spanish colonial heritage is generally important in determining when states decriminalize. The French colonial legacy is also complicated. As stated earlier, many French colonies did not receive criminalization of homosexual conduct laws from France. However, those French colonies that did have such a law have been very resistant to decriminalization. In one respect, former French colonies have a worse record than any other. Frank, Boutcher, and Camp compiled data on states that criminalized homosexual conduct after World War II.[27] Few states have enacted such laws after 1945 and three of these were former French colonies. Algeria, Cameroon, and Mauritania enacted their criminalization laws in 1966, 1972, and 1984, respectively. None of these laws were spread by French colonialism as the countries were independent at the time. So, while French imperialism cannot be held responsible for the existence of such laws, the evidence for any post-independence benefits is unclear.

The evidence in favor of the hypothesis that British colonies took longer to decriminalize, by any measure, is thus inconclusive. British colonies on average did not take longer than other colonies to decriminalize after World War II, and while they may in general have taken longer than French colonies to repeal laws after gaining independence, Spanish colonies in general took much longer. Both hypotheses H2 and H3 should thus not be accepted. In the absence of other evidence, claims that British colonialism gave a country worse prospects for decriminalizing homosexual conduct than other colonialisms are without support.

The findings presented in this chapter are somewhat at odds with related but different analyses, carried out by Asal and Sommer and Asal, Sommer, and Harwood.[28] They estimate a set of multivariate models with the aim of examining the effects of legal path dependence and religion on the likelihood of a country having a "sodomy" law on the books. One of their results is similar to the results we obtain in this chapter; that common law legal systems are far more likely to have a sodomy provision than non-common law states. However, their analysis, which includes observations on states between 1972 and 2002, also finds that common law states have been significantly less likely to repeal sodomy laws during that period. In Asal, Sommer, and Harwood, the effect that they find is large. However, in Asal and Sommer, they disaggregate legislative from court repeal and find that there is an insignificant positive effect of a common law system on court repeal (and the negative effect on legislative repeal is much smaller). It is unknown whether the inclusion of UK and Canadian decriminalization, both of which occurred before 1972, or the cases where decriminalization occurred after 2002, like Fiji, the Turkish Republic of Northern Cyprus, Nauru, Belize, or the Seychelles, or the recoding of states that did not in fact receive their law from the British, like Iraq, Sudan, Bhutan, the Maldives, etc., would alter this analysis.

Notes

1 Aengus Carroll and Lucas Ramon Mendos, "State-Sponsored Homophobia: A World Survey of Sexual Orientation Laws," *ILGA* (2017), 8.
2 http://ilga.org/ilga/en/countries/IRAN,%20ISLAMIC%20REPUBLIC%20OF/Law.
3 Robert Tielman and Hans Hammelburg, "World Survey on the Social and Legal Position of Gays and Lesbians," in *The Third Pink Book: A Global View of Lesbian and Gay Liberation and Oppression*, ed. Aart Hendriks, Robert Tielman, and Evert van der Veen (Buffalo, NY: Prometheus Books, 1993); Alok Gupta, *This Alien Legacy: The Origins of "Sodomy" Laws in British Colonialism* (New York: Human Rights Watch, 2008); David John Frank, Steven A. Boutcher, and Bayliss Camp, "The Reform of Sodomy Laws: From a World Society Perspective," in *Queer Mobilizations: LGBT Activists Confront the Law*, ed. S. Barclay, M. Berstein, and A. M. Marshall (New York: New York University Press, 2009); Douglas E. Sanders, "377 and the Unnatural Afterlife of British Colonialism in Asia," *Asian Journal of Comparative Law* 4 (January 2009): 1–49. https://doi.org/10.1017/S2194607800000417.
4 Tielman and Hammelburg, "World Survey on the Social and Legal Position of Gays and Lesbians," 251.
5 Jim Wilets, "Divergence Between LGBTI Legal, Political, and Social Progress in the Caribbean and Latin America," in *The Politics of Sexuality in Latin America: A Reader on Lesbian, Gay, Bisexual, and Transgender Rights*, ed. Javier Corrales and Mario Pecheny (Pittsburgh, PA: University of Pittsburgh Press, 2010), 249.
6 Frank, Boutcher, and Camp, "The Reform of Sodomy Laws: From a World Society Perspective."

7 Rafael LaPorta, Florencio Lopez-de-Silanes, Andrei Shleifer, and Robert Vishny, "The Quality of Government," *Journal of Law, Economics and Organization* 15, no. 1 (1999): 222–79.
8 Michael Bernhard, Christopher Reenock, and Timothy Nordstrom, "The Legacy of Western Overseas Colonialism on Democratic Survival," *International Studies Quarterly* 48, no. 1 (2004): 225–50.
9 Matthew Lange, James Mahoney, and Matthias vom Hau, "Colonialism and Development: A Comparative Analysis of Spanish and British Colonies," *American Journal of Sociology* 111, no. 5 (2006): 1412–62.
10 Daniel M. Klerman, Paul G. Mahoney, Holger Spamann, and Mark I. Weinstein, "Legal Origin or Colonial History?," *Journal of Legal Analysis* 3, no. 2 (December 1, 2011): 379–409.
11 That is by Bernhard et al. or Lange et al. as British or Spanish, or Klerman et al. as British or French. Also, if a country was identified as a colony by any of these sources, it was coded as a colony, even if only one or two sources identified it.
12 Kees Waaldijk, *Legal Recognition of Homosexual Orientation in the Countries of the World* (Leiden, Netherlands: Leiden Law School, 2009); Eddie Bruce-Jones and Lucas Paoli Itaborahy, "State-Sponsored Homophobia: A World Survey of Laws Criminalising Same-Sex Sexual Acts Between Consenting Adults," *ILGA* (2011); David John Frank, Bayliss Camp, and Steven A. Boutcher, "Worldwide Trends in the Criminal Regulation of Sex, 1945 to 2005," *American Sociological Review* 75, no. 6 (2010): 867–93.
13 Ronald Inglehart, *Culture Shift in Advanced Industrial Society* (Princeton, NJ: Princeton University Press, 1990).
14 Robert Andersen and Tina Fetner, "Economic Inequality and Intolerance: Attitudes Toward Homosexuality in 35 Democracies," *American Journal of Political Science* 52, no. 4 (2008): 942–58.
15 Cynthia Burack, *Sin, Sex, and Democracy: Antigay Rhetoric and the Christian Right* (Albany: State University of New York Press, 2008); James B. De Young, *Homosexuality: Contemporary Claims Examined in Light of the Bible and Other Ancient Literature and Law* (Grand Rapids, MI: Kregel Academic & Professional, 2000); Arno Schmitt and Jehoeda Sofer, *Sexuality and Eroticism Among Males in Moslem Societies* (Binghamton, NY: Routledge, 1992).
16 Alberto Alesina, Arnaud Devleeschauwer, William Easterly, Sergio Kurlat, and Romain Wacziarg, "Fractionalization," *Journal of Economic Growth* 8, no. 2 (2003): 155–94.
17 Ronald Inglehart and Christian Welzel, *Modernization, Cultural Change, and Democracy: The Human Development Sequence* (Cambridge: Cambridge University Press, 2005).
18 Pippa Norris and Ronald Inglehart, *Cosmopolitan Communications: Cultural Diversity in a Globalized World* (New York: Cambridge University Press, 2009).
19 "Love, Hate and the Law: Decriminalizing Homosexuality" (London: Amnesty International, 2008).
20 Helmut K. Anheier, Mary Kaldor, and Marlies Glasius, eds., *Global Civil Society 2006/7* (London: SAGE Publications Ltd, 2006).
21 James Mahoney, "Path Dependence in Historical Sociology," *Theory and Society* 29, no. 4 (2000): 507–48.
22 Michael David Sibalis, "Regulation of Male Homosexuality in Revolutionary and Napoleonic France, 1789–1815," in *Homosexuality in Modern France*, ed. Jeffrey Merrick and Bryant T. Ragan (New York: Oxford University Press, 1996), 80.

23 LaPorta, Lopez-de-Silanes, Shleifer, and Vishny, "The Quality of Government."
24 Bernhard, Reenock, and Nordstrom, "The Legacy of Western Overseas Colonialism on Democratic Survival."
25 Ibid., 243.
26 For the purpose of this analysis, those states that still have CHC laws were given an end year of 2010.
27 Frank, Boutcher, and Camp, "The Reform of Sodomy Laws: From a World Society Perspective"; Frank, Camp, and Boutcher, "Worldwide Trends in the Criminal Regulation of Sex, 1945 to 2005."
28 Victor Asal and Udi Sommer, *Legal Path Dependence and the Long Arm of the Religious State: Sodomy Provisions and Gay Rights Across Nations and Over Time* (Albany, NY: State University of New York Press, 2006); Victor Asal, Udi Sommer, and Paul G. Harwood, "Original Sin: A Cross-National Study of the Legality of Homosexual Acts," *Comparative Political Studies* 46, no. 3 (2013): 320–51.

4 Continuing criminalization of homosexuality in several former British colonies

This chapter discusses the experiences of six former British colonies that continue to criminalize homosexuality. The six countries discussed here – India, Singapore, Guyana, Jamaica, Uganda, and Kenya – are selected because of their geographical distribution across several continents, but also because of their distribution across different regime types and levels of economic development. Particularly for countries such as India, the Indian penal code of 1860 had deep implications for many other British colonies whose laws were modeled upon it. From analyses of how laws penalizing homosexual conduct were enacted during the colonial period to their contemporary modes of enforcement, this chapter ties together the similar experiences of these former British colonies and the implications these laws have had on the lives of the LGBT communities.

India

India had been lauded as the crown jewel of British Empire, and as a colony was considered indispensable for British colonial expansion in East and Southeast Asia, because of the heavy involvement of Indian soldiers in many of Britain's military campaigns, as well as its crucial location for Britain's spice and opium trade in the region. The British East Indian Company established its control in 1757, and in 1858 India was taken over to be ruled directly by the crown. Until India's independence in 1947, Britain had maintained some type of colonial rule for almost 200 years.[1]

India is the second most populous country in the world, and its population size was recently estimated at almost 1.3 billion, which is still fast growing and will surpass China in a decade.[2] It is now the seventh largest economy in the world. Although India remains overall a very poor country, with GDP per capita only at $1,709 in 2016, it nonetheless has been one of the fastest growing economies for the past few years.[3] Indian society can be characterized by its extremely diverse ethnic, linguistic and caste composition.

Although almost 80 percent of the Indian population are Hindu, there is still a substantial Muslim population at 14.2 percent, and other smaller religious denominations.[4]

During the pre-colonial era, there was "complex discourse around same-sex love and also the use, in more than one language, of names, terms, and codes to distinguish homoerotic love and those inclined to it."[5] In fact, homosexual relations had existed throughout pre-colonial India without any persecution. It was British colonial administrators who brought homophobic attitudes into India, and enshrined it through the British Law of 1860 – Indian penal code section 377.[6] The section 377 originally authored by Lord Macaulay, the president of the Indian Law Commission is still in place in India today. Section 377, entitled "Unnatural Offences," states:

> Whoever voluntarily has carnal intercourse against the order of nature with any man, woman, or animal shall be punished with imprisonment for life, or with imprisonment of either description for term which may extend to ten years, and shall also be liable to fine.[7]

It also includes an explanation, which indicates, "Penetration is sufficient to constitute the carnal intercourse necessary to the offence described in this section."[8]

It is worth noting that the law's vague use of the phrase "carnal intercourse against the order of nature" leaves room for interpretation of what exactly constitutes such acts. Different from other anti-sodomy laws in other parts of the world, the IPC section 377 does not specifically target sodomy per se. Instead, it has a biblical connotation that makes any sexual acts that do not serve the purpose of procreation liable for prosecution. Indian courts in fact have interpreted it to include other non-procreative sexual acts between men, such as oral sex, which makes criminalization of homosexual acts more pervasive.[9]

The main barrier to achieving prosecution using section 377 is that it is impractical for the police to catch people engaging in sexual acts in private.[10] Instead, Indian police historically have prosecuted homosexual men and transgender persons simply by using circumstantial evidence that they might be engaging in such sexual acts. For example, one of the historical cases of Queen-Empress v. Khairati of 1884, the police simply cited that the suspect had "distortion of the orifice of the anus into the shape of a trumpet" as incriminating evidence.[11] Although this was a historical case that occurred during the British colonial period, it nonetheless demonstrates that medical examinations and circumstantial evidences of bodily signs had been used to police homosexual men in India. There have also been many cases where police, knowing the difficulty of prosecution using section 377, instead have extorted money and/or sexual favors from gay men.[12] In addition, Indian police have the practice of using entrapment and blackmail against gay men using the threat of section 377.[13] In one case in the city of Lucknow in 2001, local police raided Naz Foundation, a local NGO, that provides support to community-based projects on male sexual health and HIV/AIDS prevention. Several activists from Naz Foundation and another group, Bharosa Trust, were arrested under section 377 on the allegation that they are "promoting homosexuality."[14] They were put in prison for 47 days, and were only released after strong domestic and international pressure.[15] Again in 2006, in the same city, local police created a fake profile on a gay dating website to lure other gay men, and arrested four men under section 377. The implications for these four gay men were devastating:

> their names, occupations and photographs were splashed all over local media. One of them, a school administrator, was fired from his job. Another left the city. Newspapers also published the name and workplace of the wife of one of the men arrested.[16]

Because of the difficulty in prosecuting consensual homosexual acts, most of the cases that have been brought under section 377 have been the ones that involve sexual assault or abuse of minors.[17] However, by equating consensual and nonconsensual sex as equivalent criminal offenses, "homosexual acts become abominable activities lacking the equivalent of 'consensual heterosexuality' and therefore incomparable."[18] Indeed, the Indian government's defense of maintaining section 377 against public pressure for decriminalization rests on a morality question. For example, in an appeal at the Supreme Court in 2005, the Indian government opined that

> even if it is assumed that the rights of sexual minorities emanate from a perceived right to privacy, it is submitted that the right to privacy cannot be extended to defeat public morality, which must prevail over the exercise of any private right.[19]

However, efforts to decriminalize homosexuality in India have been gaining momentum in the past two decades. In 1991, the New Delhi–based NGO, AIDS Bhedbhav Virodhi Andolan, issued a historical publication entitled "Less than Gay: A Citizen's Report on the Status of Homosexuality in India," which initiated a social movement in India to repeal section 377.[20] In 2001, Naz Foundation Trust filed the first public interest litigation in the Delhi High Court against section 377. Originally the Delhi High Court refused to consider this petition, but after Naz Foundation's appeal to the

Supreme Court, the case was sent back to the Delhi High Court to consider because it was related to the public interest.[21]

In July 2009, the Delhi High Court struck down the provision of section 377 in a historic judgment, on the basis that "it violated the fundamental right of life and liberty and the right to equality as guaranteed in the Constitution."[22] The court decision thus decriminalized consensual sexual relations between men, while "the provisions of Section 377 will continue to govern non-consensual penile non-vaginal sex and penile non-vaginal sex involving minors."[23] After the Delhi High Court's decision, however, several appeals were filed against it at the Indian Supreme Court by religious groups. In a 2013 decision, the Supreme Court reversed the 2009 Delhi High Court decision, thus upholding section 377, and instead ruled that such change had to occur legislatively through the parliament rather than through the court system.[24]

Finally, in February 2016, the Indian Supreme Court agreed to hear a curative appeal demanding the reversal of the decision, submitted by Naz Foundation and others.[25] While this appeal is ongoing at the time of writing, the Indian Supreme Court made a ruling that the right to privacy is a fundamental right protected by the Indian Constitution in August 2017.[26] The judges ruled that one's sexual orientation is an element of privacy and dignity.[27] Although whether section 377 will be repealed or not would need to be examined separately, some argue that this ruling "should encourage the government to act proactively and repeal this problematic penal law provision."[28] Anand Gover, who is the senior attorney representing Naz Foundation, argues that section 377 cannot stand in the face of this right to privacy rule.[29] However, the current Bharatiya Janata Party government under Narendra Modi has so far refused to repeal the law in the parliament. Most recently, on January 8, 2018, the Indian Supreme Court agreed to re-examine section 377 by saying that "A section of people or individuals who exercise their choice should never remain in a state of fear."[30] A decision is still pending. However, despite these recent legal developments, India as a whole still remains a very conservative society where homosexuality remains a taboo. According to a survey of young Indians by the Centre for the Study of Developing Societies in 2017, 61 percent of young Indians still regard homosexuality as wrong.[31]

Singapore

Singapore was founded as a free trade port city by the British in 1819 to facilitate the lucrative trade between the British Indian Company and China. Touted as a free trade city, it grew to become part of the Straits Settlements, which later became a crown colony in 1867.[32] In the post–World War II decolonization wave, Singapore initially merged with Malaysia in 1963, before it formed its own independent state in 1965 as a predominantly Chinese city-state.

Its economy grew very fast during the Cold War period. As one of the newly industrialized "tigers" in Southeast Asia, Singapore has leapt forward to be a prosperous society with a developed economy. For a city-state with a population of 5.6 million, Singapore's per capita GDP has in fact overtaken its colonial master; according to statistics from the World Bank, its GDP per capita was $52,961 in 2016, substantially more than the $39,899 of Great Britain.[33] Founded as an ethnic Chinese enclave on the Malay peninsula, Singapore's demographic composition includes three-quarters of ethnic Chinese, while Malays and Indians constitute less than 15 and 10 percent, respectively.[34] Religion wise, 33.9 percent of the population are Buddhist, 14.3 percent are Muslims, 11.3 percent are Taoist, while Catholic are 7.1 percent, Hindu are 5.2 percent, other Christians are 11 percent, and non-religious are 16.4 percent.[35]

Currently, there is only one remaining law that explicitly deals with the criminalization of homosexuality in Singapore. In 2007, Singapore's parliament repealed most of the penal code's section 377, except the section 377A. Thus, oral and anal sex between a man and woman was decriminalized, but not between two men, which means that only sex between men continues to face criminalization. Thus, currently in the Singapore penal code section 377A entitled "Outrages on Decency," notes that

> any male person who, in public of private, commits, or abets the commission of, or procures or attempts to procure the commission by any male person of, any act of gross indecency with another male person, shall be punished with imprisonment for a term which may extend to 2 years.[36]

It is worth noting that the phrase "gross indecency" was directly retained from the British Labouchere Amendments of 1885.[37] Although the current Singaporean Prime Minister Lee Hsien Loong claims that his government does not proactively enforce the section 377A anymore, nonetheless it was retained for the purpose of instigating fear among everyday homosexual life.[38] On the other hand, as reported by *The Economist*, between 2007 and 2013, a total of nine people were convicted under section 377A, according to the Singapore's State Courts' spokesperson in 2014.[39]

In addition, there are additional laws that have been used historically to police homosexuality, such as section 354 of the penal code "Outrage of Modesty," or section 294A "Obscene Act," or section 19 "Soliciting in Public Place" of the Miscellaneous Offenses in the Public Order and Nuisance Act.[40]

For example, it has been pointed out that "from 1990 to 1994, there were 50 reported cases in the newspaper of men being charged under [section 354], and the punishment was two to six months imprisonment, including three strokes of the cane."[41] Similarly, at least six cases were tried through section 294A, which caused people to be fined between 200 to 800 Singaporean dollars.[42] In 2010, one man was charged under 377A for performing oral sex on another man in a public bathroom, but he pleaded guilty to the lesser charge of committing an obscene act in public instead.[43] Additionally, between 1990 and 1994, there were 11 cases of gay men who were charged for soliciting, who were fined between 200 to 500 Singaporean dollars.[44]

There have been some challenges toward such continuation of criminalization of homosexuality in Singapore. In 2010, one man named Tan Eng Hong was arrested and charged under 377A. He later challenged the constitutionality of that provision, on the basis of the Singapore Constitution Article 12 (1) that states "All persons are equal before the law and entitled to the equal protection of the law."[45] In 2012, a gay couple, Lim Meng Suang and Kenneth Chee Mun-Leon, also filed a legal challenge. Although they had not been charged, they claimed the mere existence of this law violates their fundamental constitutional rights. On the government side, the attorney general of Singapore defended 377A, arguing that it should be up to the parliament to repeal the provision of 377A rather than the High Court. The High Court dismissed both cases after separate hearings in 2013, on the basis that the court must show deference to parliament on issues of social policy.[46] In 2014, both cases were submitted to the Court of Appeals, but were again dismissed, saying the court should not become a "mini-legislature," because "legislative functions are necessarily beyond its remit."[47]

However, it seems unlikely the Singapore legislature would be able to repeal such provisions, at least in the near future. In a speech made by Singapore Prime Minister Lee Hsien Loong, he claimed that

> Singapore is basically a conservative society . . . and the family is the basic building block of this society. And by family in Singapore we mean one man, one woman, marrying, having children and bringing up children within that framework of a stable family unit.[48]

This claim was made on the assumption that the government policies must reflect mainstream values and social norms in Singapore.[49] Indeed, according to a 2014 survey on social morality by the Institute of Policy Studies in Singapore, 78.2 percent of Singaporeans considered same-sex relations as wrong, while 72.9 percent were against gay marriage.[50] Thus, politicians can easily shift the blame to popular opinion for not pushing forward for such legal changes. When asked about his thought of the continuation of criminalization of same sex relations, Lee Hsien Loong responded that "I am prepared to live with it until social attitudes change." In fact, he claims that most Singaporeans would support keeping section 377A if there were a referendum on the statute.[51]

Continuation of criminalization aside, Singaporean society more broadly has shown some tolerance of LGBT social expression. Ever since 2009, the annual Pink Dot rallies have been organized in Singapore to show support of LGBT rights and to call for a more inclusive society where "sexual orientation represents a feature, not a barrier."[52] In 2017, the Singapore government banned foreigners from participating in the Pink Dot rally, and also banned foreign companies from sponsoring the event without a permit because it claimed that it was illegal for foreigners to participate in political protests in Singapore.[53] It has been alleged that there are foreign forces behind the gay rights movement in Singapore, and government stated that foreign entities should not interfere in domestic, political, or controversial social issues with any political overtones because "these are political, social or moral choices for Singaporeans to decide for ourselves. LGBT issues are one such example."[54] Facing the shortfall in funding because foreign companies were barred from sponsoring the event, which big multinational corporations such as Google, Twitter, and Facebook had previously funded, in the end more than 100 Singaporean companies stepped in, which allowed the organizers to surpass the fundraising target.[55] Because of the restrictions put in place, in the end, the organizers had to check IDs at the event on July 1, 2017, but more than 20,000 Singaporean citizens and permanent residents showed up to demonstrate their support for LGBT rights. Although since 2014, there has been a Wear White protest movement against the Pink Dot rallies, which has been organized by the Muslim and Christian communities, the Pink Dot rallies nonetheless have become the center of the LGBT rights movement in Singapore that has raised awareness and increased visibility for the community in Singapore. Given the status of Singapore as a regional economic hub in Southeast Asia, it is conceivable that any future improvements of LGBT rights in the country will have deep implications for other regional states.

Guyana

Located in the northern part of South America on the Atlantic coast, Guyana is the only English-speaking country on the South American continent. Originally settled by the Dutch, the territories were ceded to the British in the early 19th century, and officially became British Guyana in 1831.[56] It was ruled as a plantation economy by the British until the country gained independence in 1966 as a republic, and has remained part of the Commonwealth since then.

As a country with one of the largest rain forests in South America, Guyana is relatively sparsely populated, with a population of 800,000, and its per capita income is at 4,090 US dollars.[57] During the colonial period, the British brought many Indians to Guyana as indentured labor to work in the plantations, which explains why almost 40 percent of its population are classified as East Indians. In addition, blacks that are descendants from slavery account for almost 30 percent of the population, and the rest are several mixed categories of people.[58] There are also high levels of religious diversity in Guyana, whereby Protestant accounts for 34.8 percent, Hindu 24.8 percent, Roman Catholic 7.1 percent, Muslim 6.8 percent, and other Christians 20.8 percent.[59]

Different from other South American countries that were previously colonies of other European countries, such as the Spanish, Portuguese, or the Dutch, Guyana as a former British colony, is the only country in South America where homosexuality is still criminalized.[60] Even though Guyana achieved its independence in 1966, many of the laws have remained the same as the British colonial legal system.[61] Homosexuality is criminalized under Title 25 "Offences Against Morality" of the Guyana Criminal Law "Offences" Act Cap. 8:01.[62] Section 352 states that

> Any male person who, in public or private, commits, or is a party to the commission, or procures or attempts to procure the commission, by any male person, of any act of gross indecency with any other male person shall be guilty of a misdemeanor and liable to imprisonment for two years.[63]

Furthermore, as attempted anal sex is concerned, section 353 states that "Everyone who – (a) attempts to commit buggery; or (b) assaults any person with intent to commit buggery; or (c) being a male, indecently assaults any other male person, shall be guilty of felony and liable to imprisonment for ten years."[64] Finally, severe punishment against anal sex is listed in section 354 as "Everyone who commits buggery, either with a human being or with any other living creature, shall be guilty of felony and liable to imprisonment for life."[65] Additionally, cross-dressing is listed as a minor offense carrying a fine in the Summary Jurisdiction "Offenses" Cap. 8:02.[66]

In Guyana, although anal sex is punishable regardless of who commits it, in reality the law has generally been applied to men only.[67] As we have seen in the wording of section 352 just mentioned, it explicitly lists gross indecency as punishable for men only. Gross indecency in this instance is often interpreted as intimate acts between men other than anal sex.[68] Having said that, it seems that the Guyanese authorities do not proactively enforce the law, and it is "more common for police to use the law to intimidate men who were gay or perceived to be gay than to make arrests."[69] There have also been reports about cases where police do not actively pursue hate crimes against LGBT communities, and LGBT persons have been shunned or ridiculed by the police.[70]

In recent years, the Guyanese government has come under increasing pressure from international organizations and local civil society to decriminalize homosexuality. In February 2010, a local LGBT rights organization Society Against Sexual Orientation Discrimination (SASOD) filed a lawsuit contesting prohibition against "cross dressing," which the group claimed was "irrational, discriminatory, undemocratic, contrary to the rule of law and unconstitutional."[71] In September 2013, Guyana's Constitutional Court ruled that the country's law against cross-dressing was constitutional. However, the court did concede that as long as such an act did not constitute an "improper purpose," then there was no need to prosecute cross-dressing, which in and of itself was not a criminal offense.[72] The court nevertheless did not detail what exactly constitutes "improper purpose." The ruling was based on the idea that since the law has been in place before independence, then it is constitutionally protected from challenge, unless legislative action has been taken to invalidate that provision.[73]

In 2014, following the second cycle of Universal Peer Review under the United Nations Human Rights Council, the Guyanese government accepted three recommendations related to sexual orientation: (1) strengthen the protection of LGBT individuals; (2) take measures to ensure that hate crimes and discrimination based on sexual orientation or gender identity are vigorously investigated and appropriately prosecuted; and (3) continue its effort in eliminating discrimination against LGBT starting with the review of its related legislation. In addition, the government also noted and promised to examine another five recommendations, which are predominately on discrimination of homosexuality.[74]

Indeed, it seems there has been increasing discussion of LGBT issues in Guyana, but overall the society's attitudes towards homosexuality remain divided. For example, in a 2013 national survey, 25 percent of the respondents admitted they are homophobic, and another 18 percent supported the use of violence against LGBT persons.[75] However, in the same survey a majority of 58 percent stated they were either "tolerant" or "accepting" of homosexuals, while 17 percent were undecided.[76] Although to overcome such opposition would not be easy, it seems the general trend is toward more acceptance of LGBT rights in the country. In an interview in 2015, Guyanese President David Granger said,

> There was a times when I suppose that same-sex relations were punishable by law but in many countries those laws have been repealed so we

> have to keep abreast with what is happening in other countries but at the same time what our own people want, so try not to get ahead of the people and at the same time we try not to separate ourselves from what is taking place in the international community.[77]

In April 2017, it was revealed in a letter sent to the Inter-American Commission on Human Rights, the Guyanese government considered in order to decriminalize homosexuality, instead of relying upon legislative power, a referendum must be held. However, no such referendum is currently on the government's agenda.[78] Local LGBT organizations are also of the opinion against holding a referendum on such a divisive issue on the basis that minority rights should not be based on a popular vote. According to the Executive Director of SASOD Joel Simpson, "This divisive referendum will deepen the marginalization and isolation of LGBT persons, as right-wing groups will undoubtedly heighten their homophobic rhetoric, as is already happening on social media."[79] Thus, although social values on LGBT rights have been changing for the better in Guyana, when and how decriminalization will happen is still uncertain. Despite public opinion shifts, the colonial law clings on.

Jamaica

Located in the Caribbean, Jamaica was colonized by the British in 1655 after British troops evicted the Spanish from the island.[80] Jamaica became a slave society when the British imported more and more slaves from Africa to work in the plantations. Given the high number of slaves on the island, "race relations in Jamaica would be the most brutal in all of British America."[81] It gained independence in 1962, and remains part of the British Commonwealth.

The population of Jamaica is more than 2.8 million, with a per capita income of $4,868 in 2016.[82] Mostly as descendants from the slave trade, Jamaica's population is predominantly black at 92.1 percent, another 6.1 percent is mixed, and there are a very small number of East Indians, at 0.8 percent.[83] In terms of religion, the majority of its population are Protestant, which is about 64.8 percent of the island total, while another 21.3 percent claim to have no religious affiliation, and the rest are of much smaller denominations.[84]

Jamaica still maintains the law against homosexual conduct as per the British colonial legacy. The Jamaican Offences Against the Person Act, which was initially enacted in 1864, remains in place. It reads very similarly to the original 1861 British Offences Against the Person Act. For example, article 76 "Unnatural Crime" describes "whosoever shall be convicted of the abominable crime of buggery committed either with mankind of with any animal, shall be liable to be imprisoned and kept to hard labour for a term not exceeding ten years."[85] Article 77 then penalizes any attempt to engage in the "unnatural crime" of the previous article shall be liable to imprisonment of seven years with or without hard labor.[86] The act also clarifies that penetration alone, rather than emission, is proof of the crime. Then article 79 "Outrages on Decency" makes it illegal for male persons to commit "acts of gross indecency," which is deemed a misdemeanor offence punishable by two years in prison with or without hard labor.[87] It is worth noting that the rationale for such punishment is the denotation of such acts as "unnatural," which not only continues the rigid Victorian morality but also reflects the rejection of "same-sex intimacy as outside the boundaries of nature itself."[88]

Although these laws have rarely been enforced, they nonetheless provide an ideological justification for the prevalent societal homophobia in Jamaica, because "the very existence of sodomy laws creates a criminal class of gay men and lesbians, who are consequently targeted for violence, harassment, and discrimination because of their criminal status."[89] Indeed, in a 2006 article in the *Time Magazine*, Jamaica was described as the "most homophobic place on earth."[90] This assertion was made on the observation of the rampant violence and harassment toward LGBT persons in Jamaica. In the article, it reports one gay man was violently attacked by a gang led by a Jamaican reggae star Buju Banton, who is an avowed homophobe. In 2005, a leading gay Jamaican AIDS activist Steve Harvey was murdered by gunmen, and the previous year Jamaica's most prominent gay activist, Brian Williamson, was also murdered.[91] In a Human Rights Watch report in 2014, it described how

> LGBT Jamaicans – especially those who are poor and unable to live in safer, more affluent areas – are particularly vulnerable to violence. Many live in constant fear. They are taunted; threatened; fired from their jobs, thrown out of their homes; beaten, stoned, raped, and even killed.[92]

Worse still, many of these crimes have been left unresolved because Jamaican law enforcement has not taken "appropriate measures to prevent these attacks and to vigorously investigate and prosecute the attackers."[93]

Such violence toward LGBT people occurs amid strong societal homophobia in Jamaica. This strong homophobic social environment can be partly attributed to the strong Christian beliefs on the island, where the Church has utilized "intense 'anti-gay' advocacy and homophobic rhetoric."[94] As a majority Christian nation, the majority of these Christians also think "acceptance of LGBTQ persons is akin to turning one's back on God."[95] According to a national survey of Jamaican's attitudes towards homosexuality on a national sample of 1,000 people, 88 percent of respondents thought gays were immoral, while 83.7 percent thought the same about lesbians.[96] Pertinent to the question of criminalization of homosexual conduct, 76.7 percent of respondents did not agree to the amendment of the buggery law article 76, and only 21.3 percent claimed they would support an amendment allowing for consensual sex between adults in private.[97]

An analysis of the national survey shows that homophobia in Jamaica is statistically related with gender, age, frequency of church attendance, and education. Male, older people, frequent churchgoers, and less educated people are more likely to hold negative views toward homosexuality.[98] What is also revealing of the survey analysis is what genres of music people listen to are statistically related. It appears that people who listen to reggae and dancehall music are more likely to hold negative and hostile attitudes towards LGBT persons.[99] Indeed, people have protested against the strong homophobia among Jamaican reggae and dancehall musicians, some of whom openly called for violence towards the LGBT community.[100] Many news reports have also confirmed how homophobic lyrics in this music genre have contributed to more negative attitudes and antisocial behavior in Jamaica.[101] Indeed, the hostile social environment in Jamaica meant that progress toward decriminalization of homosexuality has been very slow. The LGBT community remains subject to high rates of harassment and discrimination.

Uganda

Uganda is a landlocked country located in the Great Lakes region of Eastern Africa. While it used to be part of British East Africa, Uganda became a British protectorate in 1894 until its independence in 1962.[102] Since its independence, the country has suffered from long periods of political chaos, from ethnic conflicts, to Idi Amin's dictatorship, to a lengthy civil war involving the Lord's Resistance Army.[103] Embroiled within regional conflicts involving its neighboring states, such as the Democratic Republic of Congo, Uganda's citizens have experienced years of mass violence.

According to a World Bank estimate in 2016, Uganda's population was 42.5 million, with a per capita income of $1,820 in terms of purchasing power parity in 2016.[104] Like most other sub-Saharan African countries, its demographic composition is extremely diverse with no ethnic group constituting more than 20 percent of the population.[105] In terms of religion, a large majority are Christians, with 45.1 percent Protestant and 39.3 percent Roman Catholic, while Muslims are about 13.7 percent.[106]

The laws that criminalized homosexuality came to Uganda after the start of British colonialism. They were formally introduced under the 1902 Order in Council, whereby British laws on "unnatural offences" started to apply in the Uganda protectorate.[107] The penal code adopted in 1950, which was developed on the basis of the Indian penal code of 1860 and the Queensland penal code, has been revised several times and currently became Cap 120. In Cap 120 section 145, it more explicitly lists the set of offenses that are categorized as "unnatural."[108] Section 145 listed the following "unnatural" offences:

> any person who – a) has carnal knowledge of any person against the order of nature; b) has carnal knowledge of an animal; or c) permits a male person to have carnal knowledge of him or her against the order of nature, commits an offence and is liable to imprisonment for life.

In addition, section 146 also says "Any person who attempts to commit any of the offences specified in section 145 commits a felony and is liable to imprisonment for seven years." Furthermore, there is section 148 that penalizes "indecent" practices, which became an offence that is liable for imprisonment of seven years.[109]

Thus, Uganda inherited those British colonial laws just in the same way as many other countries that we have discussed so far. However, instead of trying to decriminalize homosexuality, or at least not to proactively enforce it, the Uganda government instead would like to further criminalize homosexuality in the country. Already in 2005 a constitutional amendment was introduced that prohibited same-sex marriages.[110] Then in March 2009, an anti-gay workshop was organized in Kampala, the capital of Uganda, featuring several prominent evangelical Christian activists from the United States who went to Uganda to warn Ugandans about "the threat homosexuals posed to Bible-based values and the traditional African family."[111] One of the American activists, Scott Lively, seems to have played a significant role in influencing several members of the Uganda parliament, which led to an Anti-Homosexuality Act Bill to be introduced to the parliament in April that year.[112] David Bahati, who submitted the bill, claimed that Cap 120 section 145 lacks "provisions for penalizing the procurement, promoting, disseminating literature and other pornographic materials concerning the offences of homosexuality hence the need for legislation to provide for charging, investigating, prosecuting, convicting and sentencing of offenders."[113]

This notorious bill promised harsh punishment for homosexuality in the country. For the category of "offence of homosexuality," meaning people who commit various homosexual conduct, offenders would receive life imprisonment; while for the category "aggravated homosexuality," which includes sex with minors, HIV-positive status, sex through the use of drugs, and several other subcategories, they would receive the death penalty.[114] Furthermore, the bill would criminalize anyone who "aids, abets, counsels, or procures another to engage in an act of homosexuality"; they will face imprisonment of seven years.[115] The bill also would punish people for up to three years of jail if they do not report any homosexual activity to police with 24 hours, and Ugandan citizens and permanent residents breaking the law abroad will also be subject to extradition.[116] Indeed, if such a draconian bill were passed it would carry serious consequences for the LGBT communities in Uganda.

After this bill became publicly known, the country came under fierce international criticism, especially for the inclusion of the death penalty. Several Western governments threatened the cut of financial aid for Uganda if this bill became law, which was significant given how dependent the country was on such aid.[117] In the end, the parliament passed the bill in December 2013, although the death penalty was dropped in exchange for life imprisonment for both "offences of homosexuality" and "aggravated homosexuality."[118] In February 2014, President Yoweri Museveni signed the law. Immediately, the international community tabled strong criticisms toward the Ugandan government. The UN High Commissioner for Human Rights Navi Pillay, for example, denounced the law that institutionalizes criminalization of the LGBT community and could encourage harassment and violence against them.[119] The World Bank and several Western European governments, that is, Sweden, Norway, Denmark, and the Netherlands, withheld their aid/loans to the country worth US $118 million.[120] The US government also announced that some financial aid for Uganda would be withheld.[121] Furthermore, the European parliament also passed a resolution that would ban travel and visas for those responsible for the passing of the law.[122] Indeed, it seems that the passing of the law would carry serious developmental consequences for Uganda.[123] However, in August 2014, the law was struck down by the country's Constitutional Court for the lack of quorum.[124] In the end, President Museveni insisted that he would not pursue new legislation against homosexuality, and he claimed "That law was not necessary, because we already have a law which was left by the British which deals with this issue."[125]

Having said that, the demise of the new law notwithstanding, persecution against individuals based on sexual orientation and gender identity in Uganda has increased, as well as the use of harassment and violence toward the LGBT community. For example, the Ugandan government has canceled a gay pride parade in the country for two years in a row since 2016, and the Ugandan State Minister of Ethics and Integrity, Simon Lokodo, explicitly said that "It's true I ordered the police to stop and shut down all the gay pride events. No gay gathering and promotion can be allowed in Uganda. We can't tolerate it at all."[126] Meanwhile, according to a report issued by The Sexual Minorities Uganda (SMUG), there were 264 "verified cases of human rights abuses against LGBTI Ugandans" between May 2014 and December 31, 2015. And according to an interview by the SMUG representative to the *Washington Blade*, he claimed that

> When the president signed the law the citizens felt they were more empowered and they had a right to actually take action against the LGBTI people. . . . We saw a high increase of people saying, "Oh yeah I'll evict you" or "I'm evicting you from my house because the president signed the law."[127]

In fact, more and more Uganda LGBT people have fled abroad as refugees from continuation of domestic persecution. US-based organization Friends Ugandan Safe Transport Fund reported that they helped more than 1800 LGBT individuals to escape Uganda between 2014 and 2016.[128] Many of these Ugandan LGBT refugees have gone to neighboring Kenya where attitudes towards homosexuality are comparatively more tolerant.[129] Overall, it seems that the human rights situation for the LGBT community in Uganda continues to be abysmal.

Kenya

The area that later became Kenya was taken over and ruled by the British East Africa Company from 1888 as a result of growing imperial interest and British competition with Germany in the region. From 1895 to 1920 the area was ruled as a protectorate, and finally it became a crown colony in 1920. During the period of protectorate, settlers of European origin started to arrive in the temperate areas of Kenya, and later indentured labor from India also arrived to work in the construction of railways.[130] Thus after the formation of the colony there were rising tensions between the settlers and the indigenous population, which paved the way for the political violence, such as the Mau Mau rebellion in the early 1950s, that led to the independence of Kenya in 1962.[131]

Kenya is a populous country, with a population of 48.5 million, which is slightly larger than in Uganda. It is also a poor country, with a GDP per capita only at US $1,455 in 2016.[132] Similar to Uganda, Kenya also has an ethnically diverse society, where the largest ethnic group, Kikuyu, only accounts for 22 percent of the whole population, and there are numerous other smaller groups scattered across the country.[133] In terms of religion,

Christianity accounts for a large majority, with more than 83 percent of the population believing in one of a variety of Christian denominations. Also, about 11 percent of the population are Muslim.[134]

Kenya's penal code of 1930, which was put in place during the British colonial period, lists the following prohibition against homosexuality. In the section of "Unnatural Offenses," article 162 lists that

> Any person who – (a) has carnal knowledge of any person against the order of nature; or (b) has carnal knowledge of an animal; or (c) permits a male person to have carnal knowledge of him or her against the order of nature, is guilty of a felony and is liable to imprisonment for fourteen years.[135]

Although not as harsh as life imprisonment as in Uganda, Kenya's penal code article 162 also includes another item that penalizes nonconsensual sodomy to 21 years in imprisonment. Article 165 also criminalizes gross indecency among men, with the penalty being five years imprisonment.[136] Indeed, the legal prohibition against homosexuality is very severe in Kenya, which makes life as an LGBT person difficult and dangerous in the country.

Although this set of laws has not been enforced regularly, there have been cases where prosecution occurred under them. For example, in the 2006 case Francis Odingi v. Republic, Mr. Odingi was sentenced to six years in prison for having carnal knowledge of another male.[137] According to the Kenyan government, 595 cases were prosecuted under section 162 between 2010 and 2014, but most of these cases involve bestiality and rape, not consensual homosexual conduct.[138] However, the lack of frequent prosecution aside, these laws have instilled a strong sense of fear among the LGBT community and have also created a general stigma of the LGBT community within Kenyan society. In a report produced by the Kenya Human Rights Commission in 2011, after interviewing a sample of 474 Kenyans between the ages of 18 and 65, it found that human rights violations against LGBT persons were widespread and often unheeded by the Kenyan state. Additionally, the LGBT community is subject to routine abuse and violence, extortion by state officials, and overall lacks access to medical services and education.[139] The report thus calls for decriminalization of homosexuality in the country, and for the introduction of comprehensive equality and non-discrimination legislation to protect the LGBT community.[140]

In fact, Kenya passed a new constitution in 2010, which includes relatively liberal provisions, such as "the right to life, equality and freedom from discrimination, human dignity, privacy, and freedom of expression."[141] It thus seems one can interpret that the existing laws criminalizing homosexuality might be unconstitutional. At least it would seem there will be room for litigation to repeal these laws based on such constitutional provision. In the 2010 universal periodic review (UPR) for Kenya, recommendations were given by the United States and several European countries for Kenya to decriminalize homosexuality, but they were rejected by the Kenyan government, which cited the reason that "same sex unions were culturally unacceptable."[142] Again in the 2015 cycle of UPR for Kenya, it was given the same set of recommendations to decriminalize homosexuality, and this time they were not accepted nor rejected, but noted.[143]

Although criminalization of homosexuality continues in Kenya, there have been some recent developments in the country that might signal some positive changes. For example, in 2015 Kenya's High Court ruled that an LGBT organization National Gay and Lesbian Human Rights Commission (NGLHRC) could formally register with the country's NGO coordination board.[144] Having previously rejected registration on the basis that the name of the organization was unacceptable, the High Court ruling overturned this rejection citing the decision unconstitutional because the constitution guarantees freedom of association.[145] Since then the NGLHRC has been actively involved in promoting LGBT rights in the country. In 2016, Kenya's Mombasa High Court upheld the use of anal examinations to determine a suspect's sexual orientation in a case involving two Kenyan men who were forced to do anal examinations.[146] The NGLHRC is currently representing these two men in an appeal against this discriminatory decision.[147] The organization is also in the process to submit a petition to decriminalize homosexuality in Kenya, together with six human rights defenders (the petitioners), the Kenya National Commission on Human Rights, and Katiba Institute.[148] Indeed, Eric Gitari, the executive director of NGLHRC, believes in the use of litigation methodology to challenge existing criminalization and discrimination in the Kenyan legal system.[149] The court will hear the case early in 2018, and it is difficult to anticipate what will transpire in the likely long legal battles to come.

Compared to some other African states, Kenya overall is relatively tolerant of homosexuality. These criminalization laws exist, but the state is not going out of its away to actively persecute its LGBT population. As we discussed earlier in the Ugandan case, many LGBT persons have escaped to Kenya to seek refuge because it is more tolerant than in Uganda. Having said that, the reality remains that the Kenyan society remains overall very conservative and homophobic. For example, in a global survey on attitudes toward homosexuality carried out by Pew Research Center, 90 percent of Kenyans expressed that society should not accept homosexuality, and only 8 percent thought otherwise.[150] In comparison to a similar survey carried out in 2007, the percentage of people who thought homosexuality acceptable only increased from 3 percent to 8 percent, which was still abysmally low. Given such strong social aversion toward homosexuality, it is probably unrealistic to anticipate a major legal breakthrough on the issue of decriminalization of homosexuality in Kenya yet.

Conclusion

Thus, from the review of these six selected countries around the world for the ongoing criminalization of homosexuality, we can see that the legacies of British colonialism have been long and deep. These laws, after they were introduced by the British, often simply carried over to the post-colonial periods without much change. The path-dependent legal legacies of the colonial-era law continue to haunt millions of LGBT people in these countries. Although in some of the places these laws are no longer being actively enforced, they nevertheless continue to stigmatize the LGBT community among the wider society, and prevent a more progressive development of inclusive social values. Using the excuse that such legal changes have to be done through legislative measures and are thus subject to popular opinion, the court systems in countries such as India and Singapore have remained timid in making progressive decisions. Worse still, in countries such as Jamaica and Uganda, the LGBT community face harsh treatment if caught, and their lives are under constant threat of harassment and violence. The road to the end of criminalization of homosexuality in these countries appears to remain a long and arduous one.

Notes

1 Barbara D. Metcalf and Thomas R. Metcalf, *A Concise History of Modern India*, 3rd edition (Cambridge, UK; New York: Cambridge University Press, 2012); Wilhelm Von Pochhammer, *India's Road to Nationhood: A Political History of the Subcontinent* (New Delhi: Allied Publishers, 1992).
2 "India's Population to Surpass that of China Around 2024: UN," *Times of India*, June 21, 2017.
3 World Bank Development Indicators.
4 2011 Estimate, CIA World Factbook.
5 Ruth Vanita, *Queering India: Same-Sex Love and Eroticism in Indian Culture and Society* (New York: Psychology Press, 2002), 10.
6 Ibid., 10.
7 Geetanjali Misra, "Decriminalising Homosexuality in India," *Reproductive Health Matters* 17, no. 34 (November 1, 2009): 21.
8 Ibid.
9 Alok Gupta, "Section 377 and the Dignity of Indian Homosexuals," *Economic and Political Weekly* (November 18, 2006): 4817.
10 Ibid., 4815.
11 Ibid., 4816.
12 Ibid., 4820.

13 Misra, "Decriminalising Homosexuality in India," 22.
14 "Aliens in Lucknow," *New Internationalist*, 2 June 2002.
15 Sonia Paul, "Living in Fear: LGBTs in India," *Al Jazeera*, April 17, 2014.
16 Ibid.
17 Gupta, "Section 377 and the Dignity of Indian Homosexuals," 4819.
18 Ibid., 4817.
19 Ibid., 4823.
20 The report can be accessed online at https://s3.amazonaws.com/s3.documentcloud.org/documents/1585664/less-than-gay-a-citizens-report-on-the-status-of.pdf.
21 "Gays Rights Is Matter of Public Interest: SC," *Rediff India Abroad*, February 3, 2006.
22 Nirnimesh Kumar, "Delhi High Court Strikes Down Section 377 of IPC," *The Hindu*, July 3, 2009.
23 Ibid.
24 "India Gay Sex Ruling: 'It Is a Huge Setback,'" *BBC News*, December 11, 2013.
25 "Supreme Court Agrees to Revisit Law Criminalising Homosexuality," *The Indian Express*, February 3, 2016.
26 "Indian Supreme Court in Landmark Ruling on Privacy," *BBC News*, August 24, 2017.
27 "India's Supreme Court Upholds Right to Privacy," *Human Rights Watch*, August 24, 2017.
28 Ibid.
29 "Gay Rights Activists Find New Hope as India Recognizes the Right to Privacy," *Public Radio International*, September 20, 2017.
30 Michael Safi, "India's Highest Court to Review Colonial-Era Law Criminalising Gay Sex," *The Guardian*, January 8, 2018.
31 Ibid.
32 Barbara Leitch LePoer, *Singapore: A Country Study* (Washington, DC: Library of Congress, 1991). https://archive.org/details/singaporecountry00lepo.
33 World Bank Development Indicators.
34 2016 estimate, CIA World Factbook.
35 Ibid.
36 Singapore Statutes Online, Chapter 224, Penal Code, 2008 revised edition. Accessible at http://statutes.agc.gov.sg/aol/search/display/view.w3p;page=0;query=DocId%3A%22025e7646-947b-462c-b557-60aa55dc7b42%22%20Status%3Apublished%20Depth%3A0;rec=0.
37 George Baylon Radics, "Decolonizing Singapore's Sex Laws: Tracing Section 377A of Singapore's Penal Code," *Columbia Human Rights Law Review* 45, no. 1 (2013): 57–99.
38 Michael Hor, "Enforcement of 377A: Entering the Twilight Zone," in *Queer Singapore: Illiberal Citizenship and Mediated Cultures*, ed. Audrey Yue and Jun Zubillaga-Pow (Hong Kong: Hong Kong University Press, 2012).
39 "Gay Rights in Singapore: On Permanent Parole," *The Economist*, October 31, 2014.
40 Singapore Statutes Online.
41 Laurence Leong Wai Teng, "Decoding Sexual Policy in Singapore," in *Social Policy in Post-Industrial Singapore*, ed. Lian Kwen Fee and Tong Chee Kiong (Leiden; Boston: Brill, 2008), 283.
42 Teng, "Decoding Sexual Policy in Singapore," 283.

43 Mariko Oi, "Is Singapore's Stance on Homosexuality Changing?" *BBC News*, April 23, 2013.
44 Teng, "Decoding Sexual Policy in Singapore," 283.
45 www.humandignitytrust.org/pages/OUR%20WORK/Cases/Singapore.
46 Ibid.
47 The full document of the Court of Appeal decision can be read here: www.humandignitytrust.org/uploaded/Library/Case_Law/Singapore_CA_Judgment_29.10.14.pdf.
48 Associate Press, "Singapore Reforms Sex Laws – But Not for Homosexuals," *The Guardian*, October 24, 2007.
49 Oi, "Is Singapore's Stance on Homosexuality Changing?."
50 Tham Yuen-c and Maryam Mokhtar, "Singaporeans Still Largely Conservative, IPS Survey Finds," *The Straits Times*, January 28, 2014.
51 Charissa Yong, "PM Lee on BBC's Hardtalk: Most Would Back Retaining Section 377A If a Referendum Was Held," *The Straits Times*, March 1, 2017.
52 https://pinkdot.sg/about-pink-dot-sg/.
53 "Singapore LGBT Rally Says 'No Choice' But to Bar Outsiders," *BBC News*, May 15, 2017.
54 Joseph Patrick McCormick, "Singapore's Pink Dot Pride Rally Forced to Ban Foreigners," *Pink News*, May 16, 2017.
55 Linda Lakhdhir, "How LGBT Activists Are Marshaling Support From Singapore's Private Sector," *World Politics Review*, August 7, 2017.
56 Tim Merrill, ed., *Guyana and Belize: Country Studies* (Washington, DC: Library of Congress, 1992).
57 World Bank Development Indicators.
58 2012 Guyana Population & Housing Census, accessible at www.statisticsguyana.gov.gy/census.html.
59 2012 estimate, CIA World Factbook.
60 Ravin Singh, "President to Respect LGBT Rights," *Guyana Chronicle*, January 6, 2016.
61 Society Against Sexual Orientation Discrimination (SASOD) Guyana, "On Devil's Island: A UPR Submission on LGBT Human Rights in Guyana," *Sexual Rights Initiative* (2014).
62 Guyana Criminal Law Act can be accessed at www.oas.org/juridico/spanish/mesicic2_guy_criminal_law_act.pdf.
63 Ibid.
64 Ibid.
65 Ibid.
66 Society Against Sexual Orientation Discrimination (SASOD) Guyana, "Stakeholder Report to the UN Committee on Economic, Social and Cultural Rights on the Protection of the Rights of LGBTI Persons in Guyana," *Society Against Sexual Orientation Discrimination (SASOD)* (August 2015), 5.
67 "Criminalization of Homosexuality: Guyana," *Human Dignity Trust* (October 25, 2015).
68 Mahalia Jackman, "Protecting the Fabric of Society? Heterosexual Views on the Usefulness of the Anti-Gay Laws in Barbados, Guyana and Trinidad and Tobago," *Culture, Health & Sexuality* 19, no. 1 (January 2, 2017): 131.
69 "Documentation of Country Conditions Regarding the Treatment of Gay Men, Lesbians, Bisexuals, and Transgender Individuals in Guyana," *Columbia Law School Sexuality and Gender Law Clinic* (May 2017).

70 "Guyana 2014 Human Rights Report," *Country Reports on Human Rights 2014* (United States Department of State, 2014).
71 "Speaking Out: The Rights of LGBTI Citizens From Across the Commonwealth," *Kaleidoscope Trust* (2013), 42.
72 "Criminalization of Homosexuality: Guyana."
73 Ibid.
74 The UPR database on Guyana can be accessed online at www.upr-info.org/database/index.php?limit=0&f_SUR=71&f_SMR=All&order=&orderDir=ASC&orderP=true&f_Issue=All&searchReco=&resultMax=300&response=&action_type=&session=&SuRRgrp=&SuROrg=&SMRRgrp=&SMROrg=&pledges=RecoOnly.
75 Society Against Sexual Orientation Discrimination (SASOD) Guyana, "On Devil's Island: A UPR Submission on LGBT Human Rights in Guyana," 4.
76 "Guyanese Are Largely Either Tolerant Or Accepting of Homosexuals," *Kaieteur News*, July 23, 2013.
77 Tracey Khan-Drakes, "Granger Says His Beliefs Will Not Affect Decisions on Secular Issues," *Inews Guyana*, May 27, 2015.
78 "No Referendum on Same-Sex Intimacy – Harmon," *Guyana Times*, June 3, 2017.
79 Ibid.
80 William James Gardner, *The History of Jamaica: From Its Discovery by Christopher Columbus to the Year 1872* (New York: Routledge, 2005), 27–8.
81 Bernard Bailyn and Philip D. Morgan, *Strangers Within the Realm: Cultural Margins of the First British Empire* (Chapel Hill: UNC Press Books, 2012), 174–5.
82 World Bank Development Indicators.
83 2011 estimate, CIA World Facebook.
84 Ibid.
85 Full text of the Jamaica Offenses Against the Person Act can be accessed online at http://cda.gov.jm/sites/default/files/content/Offences%20Against%20the%20Person%20Act.pdf.
86 Ibid.
87 Ibid.
88 Joseph Gaskin Jr., " 'Buggary' and the Commonwealth Caribbean: A Comparative Examination of the Bahamans, Jamaica, and Trinidad and Tobago," in *Human Rights, Sexual Orientation and Gender Identity in the Commonwealth* (London: University of London, 2013), 432.
89 Christopher R. Leslie, "Creating Criminals: The Injuries Inflicted By Unenforced Sodomy Laws," *Harvard Civil Rights-Civil Liberties Law Review* 35, no. 1 (2000): 103.
90 Tim Padgett, "The Most Homophobic Place on Earth?," *Time Magazine*, April 12, 2006.
91 "Jamaican Gay Activist Shot Dead After Being Abducted," *The Guardian*, December 6, 2005.
92 "Not Safe at Home: Violence and Discrimination Against LGBT People in Jamaica," *Human Rights Watch* (October 21, 2014).
93 "Human Rights Violations Against Lesbian, Gay, Bisexual, and Transgender (LGBT) People in Jamaica: A Shadow Report," *J-FLAG; Women's Empowerment for Change (WE-Change); The Colour Pink Foundation; TransWave; Center for International Human Rights, Northwestern Pritzker School of Law of Northwestern University; Global Initiatives for Human*

Rights of Heartland Alliance for Human Needs & Human Rights (October 2016), 2.

94 Delores E. Smith, "Homophobic and Transphobic Violence Against Youth: The Jamaican Context," *International Journal of Adolescence and Youth* (June 15, 2017): 3.

95 Roxy Rezvany, "The Challenges of Running a Queer Homeless Shelter in Jamaica," *Vice*, March 22, 2016.

96 Department of Sociology, Psychology and Social Work, University of West Indies, Mona, "National Survey of Attitudes and Perceptions of Jamaicans towards Same Sex Relationships," *J-FLAG; AIDS-Free World* (2012), 2.

97 Ibid.

98 Ibid., 27–9.

99 Ibid., 28.

100 Keon West and Noel M. Cowell, "Predictors of Prejudice Against Lesbians and Gay Men in Jamaica," *The Journal of Sex Research* 52, no. 3 (March 24, 2015): 296–305.

101 Keon West, "Why Do So Many Jamaicans Hate Gay People?" *The Guardian*, June 6, 2014.

102 Ian Leggett, *Uganda* (Oxford: Oxfam, 2001), 81.

103 Phares Mukasa Mutibwa, *Uganda Since Independence: A Story of Unfulfilled Hopes* (London: C. Hurst & Co. Publishers, 1992).

104 World Bank Development Indicators.

105 2014 estimate, CIA World Factbook.

106 Ibid.

107 Adrian Jjuuko, "The Incremental Approach: Uganda's Struggle for the Decriminalisation of Homosexuality," in *Human Rights, Sexual Orientation and Gender Identity in the Commonwealth: Struggles for Decriminalisation and Change* (London: Institute of Commonwealth Studies, School of Advanced Study, University of London, 2013), 386.

108 Ibid., 386–7.

109 The whole penal code can be accessed at www.wipo.int/wipolex/en/text.jsp?file_id=170005.

110 Jjuuko, "The Incremental Approach: Uganda's Struggle for the Decriminalisation of Homosexuality," 382.

111 Jeffrey Gettleman, "Americans' Role Seen in Uganda Anti-Gay Push," *The New York Times*, January 3, 2010.

112 Mariam Black, "Meet the American Pastor Behind Uganda's Anti-Gay Crackdown," *Mother Jones*, March 10, 2014.

113 www.publiceye.org/publications/globalizing-the-culture-wars/uganda-antigay-bill.php#april.

114 Ibid.

115 Ibid.

116 Ibid.

117 "Uganda Minister Says Gay Death Penalty 'Unnecessary,'" *BBC News*, January 8, 2010.

118 "Ugandan MPs Pass Life in Jail Anti-Homosexual Law," *BBC News*, December 20, 2013.

119 www.ohchr.org/EN/NewsEvents/Pages/DisplayNews.aspx?NewsID=14275&.

120 Drazen Jorgic and Philippa Croome, "New Law Drives Uganda's Embattled Gays Deeper into Shadows," *Reuters*, March 9, 2014.

121 Jorgic and Croome, "New Law Drives Uganda's Embattled Gays Deeper into Shadows."
122 "Europe Backs Sanctions Over Anti-Gay Laws," *Al Jazeera*, March 13, 2014.
123 Tristan Regan, *Uganda's Anti Homosexuality Act 2014: A Perspective on the Developmental Consequences* (Aalborg, Denmark: Aalborg University, 2014).
124 "Uganda Anti-Gay Law Declared 'Null and Void' by Constitutional Court," *The Guardian*, August 1, 2014.
125 "Uganda's President Says New Anti-Gay Laws 'Not Necessary,'" *Pink News*, September 16, 2015.
126 Samuel Okiror, " 'No Gay Promotion Can Be Allowed': Uganda Cancels Pride Events," *The Guardian*, August 21, 2017.
127 Michael Lavers, "Report: Anti-LGBT Persecution Increased Under Uganda Law," *Washington Blade*, April 22, 2016.
128 Rachel Banning-Lover, "Where Are the Most Difficult Places in the World to Be Gay or Transgender?," *The Guardian*, March 1, 2017.
129 Daniel Wesangula, "On the Run From Persecution: How Kenya Became a Haven for LGBT Refugees," *The Guardian*, February 23, 2017.
130 www.historyworld.net/wrldhis/PlainTextHistories.asp?historyid=ad21.
131 Nick van der Bijl, *The Mau Mau Rebellion: The Emergency in Kenya 1952–1956* (Barnsley, South Yorkshire: Pen & Sword Military, 2017).
132 World Bank Development Indicators.
133 CIA World Factbook.
134 Ibid.
135 Records of Kenya's Penal Code can be accessed at www.kenyalaw.org/Downloads/GreyBook/8.%20The%20Penal%20Code.pdf.
136 Ibid.
137 Courtney E. Finerty, "Being Gay in Kenya: The Implications of Kenya's New Constitution for Its Anti-Sodomy Laws," *Cornell International Law Journal* (2012): 432.
138 Anna Dubuis, "Kenya Could Become the Next Country in Africa to Legalize Homosexuality," *Vice News*, May 10, 2016.
139 Kenya Human Rights Commission, "The Outlawed Amongst US: A Study of the LGBTI Community's Search for Equality and Non-Discrimination in Kenya" (Nairobi, Kenya, 2011), 1–2.
140 Ibid., 51.
141 Finerty, "Being Gay in Kenya: The Implications of Kenya's New Constitution for Its Anti-Sodomy Laws," 432.
142 "Kenya: Submission to the Universal Periodic Review," *Human Rights Watch*, June 16, 2014. For the full response made by the Kenyan government to the list of recommendations given at the UPR, see www.upr-info.org/sites/default/files/document/kenya/session_8_-_may_2010/recommendationstokenya2010.pdf.
143 For details of the 2015 UPR on Kenya, see www.upr-info.org/sites/default/files/document/kenya/session_21_-_january_2015/recommendations_and_pledges_kenya_2015.pdf.
144 "Kenya: High Court Orders LGBT Group Registration," *Human Rights Watch*, April 28, 2015.
145 Ibid.

146 "Kenya Upholds Use of Anal Exam to Determine Sexual Orientation," *The Guardian*, June 16, 2016.
147 www.nglhrc.com/litigation#our-wins.
148 Ibid.
149 "Kenya: Turning the Tide for LGBT Rights in Kenya," *All Africa*, March 7, 2017.
150 Pew Research Center, "The Global Divide on Homosexuality" (2013), 1.

5 Decriminalization of homosexuality in several former British colonies

This chapter discusses the experiences of six former British colonies that have successfully decriminalized homosexuality in the recent past. These five countries and one territory (in Hong Kong's case after its reversion to Chinese sovereignty in 1997) discussed here – Hong Kong, South Africa, Cyprus, Fiji, Belize, and Seychelles – are selected because of their geographical distribution across several continents, but also because of their distribution across different regime types and levels of economic development. From analyses of how laws penalizing homosexual conduct were enacted during the colonial period to the political processes and circumstances under which decriminalization occurred, this chapter ties together the similar but varying experiences of these former British colonies and the implications that decriminalization has had on the lives of those in LGBT communities.

Hong Kong

As an island offshore composed mainly of a few fishing villages, the Hong Kong island was ceded by China's last Qing Dynasty to Britain after the former's defeat in the First Opium War in 1842. Kowloon was later ceded to Britain in 1860, and the New Territories were leased by China to Britain for 99 years in 1898. Thus, by the end of the 19th century, all the territories that constitute contemporary Hong Kong came under British rule.[1] Throughout the years, the crown colony became the main entrepôt for British trade with China. Except during eight years of Japanese occupation during World War II, British rule lasted until 1997 when Hong Kong was finally returned to Chinese sovereign rule under the One Country Two Systems model.

As an economically developed city-state, Hong Kong has a population of 7.4 million, and a GDP per capita of US $43,681 according to a World Bank estimate in 2016.[2] Ethnic Chinese enjoy an overwhelming majority of the city's population at 93.1 percent, as a result of migration from Mainland China due to years of warfare and political instability.[3] In terms of religion, other than about 10 percent of the population who are of the Christian faith, the majority of Hong Kong's population believes in a mixture of Chinese folk religions such as Buddhism, Taoism, Confucianism, and so forth. After the 1997 handover, Hong Kong has enjoyed a high level of freedom including its own independent legal system through its mini-constitution, The Basic Law. Although in recent years there have been concerns over increasing interference by Beijing over Hong Kong local autonomy, Hong Kong maintains a distinct legal system that is based on a combination of British common law and local statute law, in addition to the interpretation of the basic law.[4]

During most of Hong Kong's legal history under British colonial rule, articles 49 to 53 of the Offences Against the Person Ordinance dealt directly with the criminalization of homosexuality before they were repealed in 1991.[5] For example, since 1865, article 49 specifically stated, "Any person who is convicted of the abominable crime of buggery, committed either with mankind or with any animal, shall be guilty of felony, and shall be liable to imprisonment for life."[6] Article 50 penalized attempts to buggery for imprisonment of ten years, and article 51 penalized gross indecency for two years. Further, article 52 dealt with age consent and article 53 clarified the definition of carnal knowledge between men.[7]

Different from the five country studies in the previous chapter, the process to decriminalize homosexuality in Hong Kong occurred while it was still a British Colony, and almost two decades after England and Wales decriminalized consensual homosexual conduct in the 1967 Sexual Offences Act.[8] In fact, initially there was very little demand for the colonial administration to follow suit to decriminalize homosexuality in Hong Kong after England had already done so.[9] It was only until the early 1980s that debates about homosexuality started to emerge. In 1983, the Law Reform Commission of Hong Kong issued a "Report on Laws Governing Homosexual Conduct," in which it recommended the removal of the penalty for "consensual sexual conduct between not more than two males in total privacy, and provided both are over 21 years of age."[10] Despite such recommendations, the colonial administration chose not to implement the decriminalization, citing opposing public opinion on issues of homosexuality.[11]

The process for decriminalization of homosexuality in Hong Kong has to be understood within the broad political context prior to Hong Kong's handover in 1997. After the 1985 Joint Declaration between China and the United Kingdom that set in motion Hong Kong's imminent handover, there was high anxiety among the local population about the uncertain future of living under Chinese rule where the Chinese Communist Party monopolizes political power. Particularly after the 1989 Tian'anmen incident, Hong Kong society was shocked by the brutal suppression of the student democracy movement in Beijing, and strong fears grew about its own future after 1997.[12] As a result, the colonial government decided to introduce human rights legislation to allay public concern, a draft of which was released in March 1990.[13] During the consultation process, mood at the Hong Kong Legislative Council (LegCo) was such that only a strong Bill of Rights can guarantee Hong Kong's autonomy and increase people's confidence about Hong Kong's future, so that a smooth transition to handover to Chinese rule can be maintained.[14]

It was during this process of public consultation for the Bill of Rights that defense against the continued criminalization of homosexuality became untenable. It was argued by the pro-decriminalization members of LegCo that continued criminalization of homosexuality would come under legal challenge when the Bill of Rights was passed.[15] In the end, the motion passed 31 to 13 with six abstentions, leading the Hong Kong government to draft the Crimes (Amendment) Bill.[16] It was this legislation that got rid of articles 49 to 53 and decriminalized consensual homosexual conduct for people who are over the age of 21. Thus, the success for decriminalization was built on the general public craving for human rights protection in a Hong Kong facing imminent return to the authoritarian rule of Beijing. Later, the age of consent for homosexual conduct was lowered to 16 in 2014 after a lengthy judicial review. However, currently there is unequal treatment between vaginal intercourse and buggery for sex with underage persons, and a legal appeal has been made to change that.[17]

Decriminalization aside, there is still a lack of comprehensive legislation against discrimination based on sexual orientation in Hong Kong. In 1994, Legislative Councilor Anna Wu proposed a comprehensive Equal Opportunity Bill, with a long list of prohibitions of discrimination, including on the basis of sexual orientation.[18] However, the government in the end passed its own version of Sex Discrimination Bill, which dropped sexual orientation from the list.[19] Although later the Home Affairs Bureau published a "Code of Practice Against Discrimination in Employment on the Ground of Sexual Orientation," calling for both employers and employees to eliminate discriminatory practices in employment, it was nonetheless a non-enforceable recommendation rather a legally binding law.[20] Certainly the issuance of such a code of practice is commendable, without the punitive power of a law, self-regulation would not be as effective in eliminating these long-held prejudice and discrimination against the LGBT community. Indeed, in March 2017, Hong Kong's equality watchdog Equal Opportunities Commission issued a statement with the support of 75 major organizations calling for a legislation against discrimination on the grounds of sexual orientation, gender identity and intersex status, claiming that without such a legislation "the city was losing its competitive edge in the global talent contest."[21]

This concern that Hong Kong is losing its competitive edge is partly due to the fact that many Western countries have already made fast-paced legal changes to accommodate sexual minorities. In an online survey conducted by Dr. Yiu-tung Suen at Chinese University of Hong Kong with 1,026 LGBT people in Hong Kong in August 2016, it was reported that

> 39 per cent had considered leaving Hong Kong because of the lack of legal protection against discrimination on the grounds of sexual orientation; 48 per cent had considered leaving because same-sex marriage was not legalised or recognised in Hong Kong; and 26 per cent had considered leaving because of the difficulties facing same-sex partners who wanted children.[22]

Indeed, in the age where same sex marriage has become legalized in more and more countries, Hong Kong's existing legal provision has become inadequate in dealing with such new development. There have been a couple of recent court cases that are challenging the current definition of marriage between a man and woman according to Hong Kong's Basic Law. The first case is a Hong Kong immigration officer who married his male partner in New Zealand in 2014, started a legal campaign against the Hong Kong government, claiming that his husband should be entitled to the same benefits available to heterosexual couples. In April 2017, the High Court ruled against the Hong Kong Civil Service Bureau, with Justice Anderson Chow Ka-ming stating,

> I am unable to see how denial of "spousal" benefits to homosexual couples . . . legally married under foreign laws could or would serve the purpose of not undermining the integrity of the institution of marriage in Hong Kong, or protecting the institution of the traditional family.[23]

Another case was a British lesbian couple who entered a civil union partnership in England in 2011, but one of them got her spousal visa denied by Hong Kong Immigration Department which refused to recognize legal same-sex partnership. In September 2017, Hong Kong's Court of Appeal ruled against the immigration authorities, stating that the current visa regime "failed to justify the indirect discrimination on account of sexual orientation."[24] In both cases, the Hong Kong government has not accepted the rulings, but is still in the process of appeal.

Despite the lack of enough progress on the part of the Hong Kong government, general social attitudes toward the LGBT community have changed significantly from the past. For example, according to a recent study commissioned by Hong Kong's Equal Opportunity Commission, almost 56 percent of the surveyed reported that they would support legislation against discrimination on the grounds of sexual orientation.[25] In October 2017, Hong Kong also won the opportunity to host the 2022 Gay Games, the first time in Asia. The Hong Kong Tourism Board has been reported saying that they would support this event and they were pleased Hong Kong had been selected which proved "the city could be a major destination for 'a rich diversity' of events."[26] It is thus reasonable to hope that with time Hong Kong will become more inclusive and tolerant of the LGBT community in this cosmopolitan city.

South Africa

The Cape of Good Hope first became a colony of the Dutch East India Company in the mid-17th century. The territory was first annexed by the British in 1806 and then transferred to Britain in 1815 after a treaty between the United Kingdom and the Netherlands.[27] After Britain's victory in the Boer War, the whole of South Africa came under British rule as a dominion of the Union of South Africa in 1910, and the country was allowed self-government in 1931. In 1961, South Africa became a republic and left the British Commonwealth. The modern history of South Africa has been plagued by its white minority domination that set up an apartheid regime that deprived its black citizens of their fundamental rights. It was not until 1994 that apartheid ended, and the African National Union under the leadership of Nelson Mandela formed a democratic government on the basis of racial equality.

With a population of 55.9 million, South Africa has a GDP per capita of US $5,273 in 2016.[28] As an ethnically and racially diverse society, South Africa's census reports that 76.4 percent of its population are Africans, 9.1 percent white, 8.9 percent colored, and 2.5 percent Asians.[29] The South African government also recognizes more than ten official languages, which demonstrates how the emphasis on diversity and equality has defined the post-apartheid South Africa.[30] In terms of religion, Christianity of various denominations is the predominant majority with less than 20 percent of its population who are not Christian.[31]

Different from other cases that we cover in this book, it was the Dutch but not the British who first introduced the sodomy law into the Cape colony in the 17th century.[32] This version of Roman-Dutch law continued in South Africa despite the fact that in the Netherlands sodomy was decriminalized after the imposition of the Napoleonic legal code in 1811. In the Dutch-Roman common law, sodomy was categorized among the list of "unnatural offenses" that include non-procreative sexual acts between men, women, bestiality, heterosexual anal intercourse, and masturbation.[33] After the

British took over the Cape colony, the British mostly retained the existing penal code. Additionally, "with the increasing introduction of English common law in the 19th and 20th centuries, sodomy gradually became restricted to unlawful sexual intercourse *per anum* (anal intercourse) between human males."[34] Thus, were South Africa to be continually ruled under the Dutch rather than the British, criminalization of sodomy probably would have been modified or rejected much earlier.[35]

The criminalization of homosexuality was deeply associated with the apartheid regime that had deep roots in the Afrikaner nationalism and Calvinism.[36] Policing of "unnatural offences" such as homosexual acts had been motivated by the need of the apartheid regime to "keep the white nation sexually and morally pure so that it had the strength to resist the black communist onslaught."[37] The infamous Immorality Act of 1957, implemented during the apartheid period, was a piece of legislation that aimed to curb relationships between people. In addition to prohibiting sexual intercourse between people of different racial and ethnic backgrounds, it also penalized "unnatural and immoral sexual acts," which was a euphemism for homosexual conduct. Although the enforcement of this law was relatively slack, the police nonetheless harass the LGBT community using the excuse of this law.[38] In 1966, amendments were made to the Immorality Act that increased the consent age from 16 to 19, and outlawed dildos.[39] In addition, it included an infamous "three men at a party clause," which criminalized "any man who commits with another male person at a party 'any act which is calculated to stimulate sexual passion or to give sexual gratification.' The provision defines party as 'any occasion where more than two persons are present.'"[40]

Political activism to decriminalize homosexuality was closely associated with the broader context of anti-apartheid political mobilization. In the 1980s, two prominent LGBT organizations – Gay and Lesbian Organization of the Witwatersrand (GLOW) and Organization of Lesbian and Gays Activists (OLGA) – were formed to showcase the LGBT movement in South Africa and started to embrace a nonracial and democratic character, while also calling for an end of all forms of discrimination.[41] More importantly, in 1987 the African National Congress (ANC) also started to accept LGBT rights as part of its liberation struggle.[42] Indeed, it was claimed that contacts between high-profile ANC members and LGBT activists during these years were fundamental for the inclusion of a prohibition of discrimination on the grounds of sexual orientation in the ANC's proposal of the Bill of Rights.[43] Thus, the interim constitution of 1994, which ended apartheid, included an equality clause with "sexual orientation" in it.[44] As a result of this interim constitution, a National Coalition for Gay and Lesbian Equality (NCGLE) was formed to push for the inclusion of "sexual orientation" in the final version of the constitution.[45] Emphasizing the commonality between discrimination on the grounds of sexual orientation with those on race or gender, NCGLE mobilized a powerful framework on LGBT rights in post-apartheid South Africa.[46] Thus through the 1996 constitution, South Africa became the first country in the world that explicitly outlawed discrimination on the grounds of sexual orientation.[47]

Despite this constitutional change that protected the LGBT community from discrimination, the previous law criminalizing homosexual conduct was nonetheless still on the books. In 1998, the Constitutional Court ruled in the case *NCGLE v. Minister of Justice* to finally strike down sodomy as a crime.[48] According to the judgment of Justice Ackermann, the sodomy laws violated the LGBT person's constitutional rights to dignity, privacy, and equality.[49] In the ruling, explicit comparison between discrimination on the grounds of race and sexual orientation was made.[50] This indicates how in the post-apartheid South Africa, the emphasis of equality has reached such a commanding level because of its past injustice of racial segregation and discrimination that all other related issues of inequality have become the core of the country's transitional justice process.

Indeed, more positive rights for the South African LGBT community were to come. In December 1999, the Constitutional Court ruled long-term same-sex partners of South African citizens or permanent residents should be treated as spouses when immigration is concerned.[51] In separate court rulings in 2002, long-term same-sex partners were granted rights to pensions of their deceased partners, same-sex couples were allowed to adopt children, and same-sex couples were allowed to be registered as parents for children born to one of them.[52] Then in December 2005, the Constitutional Court ruled unanimously that the common law definition of marriage as between one man and one woman was unconstitutional, and the existing Marriage Act was invalid.[53] Then in December 2006, the South African government passed the Union Bill, which legalized same-sex marriage, which made South Africa the first country in Africa to do so.[54] Thus, legally, homosexual persons in South Africa achieved full parity with heterosexual persons for the first time in history.

Despite all the progresses in legal rights for the LGBT community in South Africa, homophobia and discrimination persist. One of the most disturbing problems is the prevalence of corrective rapes against lesbian women.[55] Given the overall high levels of crime rates in South African society, the LGBT communities in the country face particular risks and are often violently targeted.[56] At the same time, homophobic sentiment in South Africa continues to frame homosexuality as "unAfrican," "unGodly," and "unnatural."[57] Indeed, more needs to be done to combat these persistent social prejudices in a country that has otherwise made huge stride toward achieving equality among people.

Cyprus

Britain acquired control of the Island of Cyprus in 1878 through the Convention of Cyprus while the island remained nominally under the sovereignty of the Ottoman Empire. After the outbreak of the First World War, Britain formally annexed Cyprus, and made it a crown colony in 1925.[58] During the colonial period, the British created a "divide and rule" system to manage the relations between the Greek and Turkish parts of Cyprus, which set in motion the conflicts between the two communities in the years to come.[59] In 1960, Cyprus achieved its independence from British rule as a republic. However, the post-independent Cyprus descended into intercommunal violence between the Greek Cypriot and Turkish Cypriot communities on the island that led the United Nations send in a peacekeeping mission to the island. The United Nations Peacekeeping Force in Cyprus has remained stationed there ever since.[60] In 1975, the northern part of the island was proclaimed a Turkish Federated State of Cyprus, which changed its name in 1983 to the Turkish Republic of Northern Cyprus. However, Northern Cyprus was not recognized as an independent state by the international community with the exception of Turkey.[61] In 2004, Cyprus became part of the European Union, but the separation between the south and north continues.

As a small island nation, Cyprus has a population of 1.17 million, of which the Greek part is about 850,000, and the Turkish part is slightly over 300,000. The per capita income overall is US $23,324 according to World Bank estimates in 2016.[62] Because the island is under the control of two separate governments, ethnic and religious divisions fall closely along the line between the Greek and Orthodox Christian and Turkish and Muslim parts of Cyprus society. Indeed, even the legal process of decriminalization of homosexuality fell along the same line of division.

The effect of British colonialism on the criminalization of homosexuality is explicitly clear in the Cyprus case. Before it officially became a crown colony in 1925, Cyprus had followed Ottoman laws, which by that time had decriminalized homosexuality. The Ottoman Empire during the Tanzimat period of the mid-19th century had already adopted "the Napoleonic Trade Laws in 1850, the French Penal Code in 1858, the Property Law in 1858, and the Maritime Trade Law in 1864."[63] Thus, by adopting the French penal code in 1858, which had already got rid of the sodomy law, the Ottoman Empire had decriminalized homosexuality, including in Cyprus. However, after it became a British colony, homosexuality became recriminalized again. According to section 171 of the criminal code of Cyprus enacted in 1929,

> Any person who (a) has carnal knowledge of any person against the order of nature, or (b) permits a male person to have carnal knowledge

> of him against the order of nature is guilty of a felony and is liable to imprisonment for five years.[64]

In 1989, a Cyprus citizen, Mr. Alecos Modinos, filed a case against the Cyprus government at the European Court of Human Rights on the basis that the criminalization of homosexuality in the Cyprus penal code constituted a violation of the Convention for the Protection of Human Rights and Fundamental Freedoms (Convention) on the basis of interference of his rights to privacy.[65] The Cyprus government at the time had not enforced the penal code section 171 since 1981 after the judgment of the European Court in the Dudgeon v. The United Kingdom case, which decriminalized homosexuality in Northern Ireland and had wide implications for setting the legal precedent against the criminalization of homosexuality in the Council of Europe.[66] However, since that ruling, its various ministers of justice had stated publically that the Cyprus government was not in favor of amending the law.[67] In the end the European Court of Human Rights ruled in favor of Mr. Modinos that the existing prohibition of homosexuality in the Cyprus penal code was a breach of article 8 of the convention that states, "Everyone has the right to respect for his private and family life, his home and his correspondence."[68] Thus, consensual homosexual conduct in private in Cyprus were decriminalized through the European Court of Human Rights.

However, despite the ruling, the Cyprus government did not immediately amend its penal code. In fact, its domestic political battle dragged on all the way until 1998, only a few days before the ultimatum set by the Council of Europe.[69] The government, keen to join the European Union, had pressed the legislature to pass an amendment bill for two years. However, the legislators were worried about the electoral repercussions and particularly the vehement objection by the Orthodox Church of Cyprus.[70] For example, the Archbishop Chrysostomos spoke out in strongest terms against decriminalizing homosexuality, saying that "The Church condemns homosexuality as a sinful and repulsive act because it is contrary to the spirit of Scripture and the law of nature."[71] In the end, the Cyprus House of Representatives passed the amendment with 36 votes for and 8 against, with a clear concern about the implications for Cyprus' relations with Europe if the amendment did not get passed.[72] Yet, there were still strong resistances to treat the LGBT community equally in law. For example, the age of consent for homosexuals was 18 years while for heterosexuals was 16. It wasn't until 2002 that the age of consent for both homosexuals and heterosexuals were equalized to be 17.[73]

Although the southern part of the Cyprus under the control of the Cyprus government decriminalized homosexuality, the Turkish Northern Cyprus had not done so until 2014. In 2012, a legal challenge was made by the Human Dignity Trust based in London on behalf of a Northern Cyprus citizen against Turkey, which represents Northern Cyprus at the European Court of Human Rights.[74] Partly prompted by this case, in January 2014, Northern Cyprus became the last territory in Europe to decriminalize homosexuality by reforming its penal code. According to lawmaker Bogus Derya, "We decriminalized homosexuality but we also changed that whole section (of the code) to modernize laws protecting human rights."[75] Thus, after the success in Northern Cyprus, according to Jonathan Cooper, the chief executive of Human Dignity Trust, "Nowhere in Europe now still criminalises gay people and we are proud to say that we have played a significant role in bringing this shameful chapter in European history to an end."[76]

Since Cyprus became a member of the European Union in 2004, its domestic laws have also been brought in line with EU laws. For example, its Equal Treatment in Employment and Occupation Law in 2004 was the first of antidiscrimination legislation that included sexual orientation.[77] In 2013, the country's penal code was reformed to include protection against violence and hate speech on the basis of sexual orientation and gender identity. The new amendment criminalizes any person who commits such discrimination on the

> basis of sexual orientation or gender identity, is guilty of an offence and in case of conviction is subject to imprisonment not exceeding three years or to a fine not exceeding €5,000 (£4250) or to both such a fine and imprisonment.[78]

Although there is still no legalized same sex marriage in Cyprus, the government in 2015 approved civil partnership, which allowed people of any sexual orientation to form civil partnerships to regulate their property and alimony.[79] It is reported that in 2016, about 70 gay or lesbian couples entered into such civil partnerships.[80] Social attitudes toward homosexuality are also slowly progressing, although they are still overall very conservative. For example, the 2006 Eurobarometer found that 14 percent of Cypriots agreed that same sex marriage should be allowed.[81] However, according to research conducted in February 2014, "53.3 per cent of Cypriot citizens accept civil partnership legislation."[82] Certainly civil partnership is substantially different from same sex marriage, but at least it seems that conservative social attitudes in Cyprus are changing. Having said that, the Orthodox Church in Cyprus remains one of the biggest anti-LGBT rights forces in the southern part of the country,[83] which means there are still long battles ahead for equal rights for LGBT communities in Cyprus.

Fiji

Composed of an archipelago of more than 300 islands in the South Pacific, Fiji became a colony of Great Britain after it was ceded by a group of chiefs.[84] The British were interested in growing cotton and sugar cane in Fiji, and brought over laborers, many of whom came from India, to work in these plantations. During the colonial period, these Indian laborers and the indigenous Fijian population were managed separately because the British did not want to interfere with the local way of life and thus did not use indigenous labor. The numbers of indentured laborers from India grew until, by the time Fiji gained its independence in 1970 as a Commonwealth Realm, it was left with a legacy of a bipolar ethnic polity. The divide between the indigenous population and the almost equally numerous imported laborers meant ethnic strife between these two communities during the post-independent period.[85] In 1987 Fiji became a republic after two military coups, after which many people of Indian origin emigrated from Fiji due to the civil unrest targeted at them by Fijian indigenous nationalists.

Fiji's population is relatively small. According to the estimate by the World Bank in 2016, the total population of this island nation is less than 900,000 people, and its GDP per capita in 2016 was $5,153.[86] Its demographic composition, as mentioned earlier, is more bipolar, in that ethnic Indians comprise about 37.5 percent while the indigenous group iTaukei is about 56.8 percent.[87] Religious beliefs also fall roughly along the ethnic divisions. There is about 27.9 percent and 6.3 percent of the people in Fiji believe in Hinduism and Islam, respectively, and about 45 percent Protestant, 9.1 percent Roman Catholic, and 10.4 percent other Christians.[88]

Since its incorporation as a British colony, its penal code was based on Victorian-era laws prohibiting homosexual conduct. Article 175 of the Fijian penal code stated explicitly that

> Any person who (a) has carnal knowledge of any person against the order of nature; or (b) has carnal knowledge of an animal; or (c) permits a male person to have carnal knowledge of him or her against the order of nature, is guilty of a felony, and is liable to imprisonment for fourteen years, with or without corporal punishment.[89]

Additionally, article 177 allows up to five years' imprisonment for

> Any male person who, whether in public or private, commits any act of gross indecency with another male person, or procures another male person to commit any act of gross indecency with him, or attempts to procure the commission of any such act by any male person with himself or with another male person.[90]

The political process that eventually led to the decriminalization of homosexuality started with the 1997 constitution. A decade after the military coup, in 1997 Fiji adopted a new constitution that included an explicit antidiscrimination clause on the basis of sexual orientation, which made the country the second in the world, after South Africa, to have included such provision in the constitution. Article 38 of the constitution bars discrimination based on any actual or supposed personal characteristics or circumstances, including sexual orientation. Article 37 of the constitution also protects people's right to privacy.[91] Indeed, the 1997 constitution has been praised as offering a "vision of Fiji as a vibrant, multiethnic, democratic state that celebrates the indigeneity of Fiji, [and] recognizes the equal rights of all citizens."[92] It has been argued that the legacy of the civil society activism in Fiji furthered the development of LGBT rights movement in the country by promoting the inclusion of this antidiscrimination clause into the constitution.[93] Although the 1997 constitution was abolished in 2009 after a coup, the new constitution in 2013 maintained the same antidiscrimination clause.

Despite such an antidiscrimination clause in the constitution, the colonial-era law remained on the books. In 2005, a legal case involving two gay men brought this contradiction to the fore. On April 5th of that year, the Fijian Nadi Magistrate Court sentenced an Australian male and a Fijian male to two years in prison for offences "against the order or nature" and "gross indecency."[94] However, such a ruling was a direct contraction to its constitution. According to Scott Long, director of Human Rights Watch's LGBT Rights Project, "Fiji should respect its own constitutional ban on discrimination against gays and lesbians. . . . These harsh sentences are a reminder that Fiji must repeal its colonial-era sodomy laws, which threaten individuals' dignity, equality and privacy."[95] After the ruling, an appeal was raised to the High Court of Fiji, and in August 2005, the High Court overturned the previous ruling on constitutional grounds. The ruling made by Judge Gerard Winter argued that articles 175 and 177 were "inconsistent with the Constitution and invalid to the extent that this law criminalizes acts constituting the private consensual sexual conduct against the course of nature between adults."[96] Although the High Court ruling invalidated these two articles, they did not cease to exist but rather were "rendered inoperative to the extent of inconsistency."[97]

In the end, Fiji officially decriminalized consensual homosexual conduct in 2010 when its legislature passed a new national crimes decree. This made Fiji the "first Pacific Island nation with colonial-era sodomy laws to formally decriminalize sex between men."[98] According to the report by UNAIDS, wordings of "sodomy" and "unnatural acts" have been replaced with gender neutral languages. Currently in Part 12 of the National Crimes

Decree on Sexual Offenses, penalization is reserved only for rape, assault, and sex with underage persons.[99]

Although homosexuality has been decriminalized in Fiji, same-sex couples are still prevented from marriage. The existing Marriage Act explicitly states "Marriage in Fiji shall be the voluntary union of one man to one woman to the exclusion of all others."[100] Indeed, because of the strong social and political influence of the Methodist Church, Fiji politicians have come out in condemnation of the prospect of same-sex marriage in the country. For example, in 2016 Fiji's Prime Minister, Frank Bainimarama, said that "Fiji does not need that rubbish," and in fact suggested for same-sex couples who want to get married they should go to Iceland instead.[101] In 2015, the Methodist Church in Fiji made a statement on the issue, saying that "The Methodist Church in Fiji affirms its doctrinal position that marriage is a sacred covenant that is expressed in love, mutual support, personal commitment, and shared fidelity between a man and a woman."[102]

At the same time, bullying and discrimination against the LGBT community continue to happen. For example, in 2013 the spokesperson Kris Prasad of a local LGBT rights organization said in a radio interview that "There is a lot of discrimination from the state as well, especially when it comes to access to security services, as in getting access to police, and getting access to health services."[103] Having said that, overall, social attitudes toward the LGBT community have become more accepting recently.

Belize

As a Central American country, Belize, formally known as British Honduras, became a British colony in 1862, after the formation of the British Honduras Company in 1859 as a result of the British-Guatemala Treaty. Even before the establishment as a formal colony, British settlers already were engaged in the logwood industry, for which they brought thousands of slaves from Africa to work in the forests.[104] During the mid-20th century, the colony was embroiled with territorial disputes with Guatemala, with the latter claimed it as its own territory and threatened to invade several times. In 1971 the name of the country was changed to Belize in anticipation of independence. However, because of the territorial disputes with Guatemala, the country didn't achieve full independence until 1981.[105] Guatemala did not recognize Belize as an independent country until 1992.

Belize's population was estimated at 367,000 people in 2016, and its GDP per capita was $4,811 in 2016.[106] The country has a very mixed population, with 52.9 percent categorized as Mestizo, 25.9 percent as Creole, 11.3 percent as Maya, and several other ethnic groups.[107] In terms of religious beliefs, the majority follow one kind of Christianity or another. For example, about 40 percent of the population are Roman Catholics, 31.5 percent as Protestant, as well as several other much smaller denominations.[108]

Although physically located on the continent and bounded on both sides by Spanish-speaking Central American countries, Belize shares more in common with the Caribbean countries due to their similar colonial experience under the British. This meant that through most of its post-independence years the country had a legal prohibition on homosexuality like other Caribbean countries, rather than like the other Central American countries that did not have such a criminalization in place. Belize's criminal code section 53 stated that "every person who has carnal intercourse against the order of nature with any person or animal shall be liable to imprisonment for ten years."[109] This can be traced back to the criminal code of 1888, which provided that "Whoever is convicted of unnatural carnal knowledge of any person, with force or without the consent of such person, shall be liable to imprisonment with hard labour for life, and in the discretion of the Court to flogging." The 1944 amendment somehow removed the requirement of force or lack of consent, which was carried through to the post-independence criminal code.[110]

Belize's Supreme Court on August 10, 2016, declared section 53 unconstitutional, which made it the first Caribbean nation, and also the last country in Central America, to decriminalize homosexual conduct.[111] The legal battle to repeal this provision started by a Belize citizen Mr. Caleb Orozco in 2010, who is the executive director of the United Belize Advocacy Movement (UNIBAM), which is an outreach group for the LGBT community in the country.[112] Mr. Orozco filed his case against the attorney general, claiming that section 53 infringed on his constitutional rights to dignity and privacy. Section 20 of Belize's constitution granted citizen's right to see redress at the Supreme Court for any infringement of his or her fundamental rights and freedom, and section 3 specifically states that the constitution provides "protection for his family life, his personal privacy, the privacy of his home and other property and recognition of his human dignity."[113] In the end, Justice Kenneth Benjamin ruled in Mr. Orozco's favor, concurring that "Section 53 is in breach of the dignity of the claimant . . . such breach operates to inform the other rights from which the concept of human dignity emanates."[114] He also agreed that it violated Mr. Orozco's fundamental rights to privacy, and indeed he instructed the revision of Section 53 to exclude consensual sexual acts between adults, which writes "This Section shall not apply to consensual sexual adults between adults in private."[115] Indeed, as the first country in the Caribbean to strike down this law, Belize could well set up a precedent for other former British colonies in the Caribbean, and we will probably see more legal challenges in these countries in the years to come.[116]

Overall, social attitudes toward the LGBT community in Belize are relatively tolerant. According to a survey done by UNAIDS in 2013 with 773 persons in Belize between the ages of 18 and 64, 34 percent said that they accept someone who is gay or homosexual and another 34 percent said they would tolerate someone who is gay or homosexual. According to Ernest Massiah, regional director of UNAIDS Caribbean, this statistic is higher than other East Caribbean countries, and "Belize is really showing itself to be a more accepting society," and there are also "high levels of support for anti-discrimination legislation."[117] And indeed, the first gay pride parade was held in August 2017 in Belize, one year after the decriminalization court ruling.

On the other hand, Belize bizarrely has an immigration ban of homosexuals to the country. Section 5 (1C) of its Immigration Act states that "any prostitute or homosexual or any person who may be living on or receiving or may have been living on or receiving the proceeds of prostitution or homosexual behaviour" are prohibited from immigration to Belize.[118] In 2013, a LGBT activist from Jamaica Mr. Maurice Tomlinson filed a case against the government of Belize and Trinidad and Tobago at the Caribbean Court of Justice (CCJ), claiming that his right of free movement within the Caribbean Community (CARICOM) had been prejudiced.[119] In June 2016, the CCJ ruling dismissed Mr. Tomlinson's case on the basis that this immigration ban is not enforced, and Mr. Tomlinson's freedom of movement within the CARICOM has already been guaranteed and thus he has no valid reason to feel being prejudiced.[120]

At the same time, there are conservative religious groups in Belize that have been organizing to push back some of the legal progress that have been made in the country. Right after Mr. Orozco's victory, the National Evangelical Association of Belize filed court papers to appeal the ruling. Similarly, the Catholic church has also made the appeal. The two major church organizations have also been working on proposals of Constitutional Amendments to protect "traditional marriage and family."[121] Although the churches' appeal was rejected by the court because they were not the original interested party to the case, the government of Belize decided to file a partial appeal in the Caribbean Court of Justice. It wants the interpretation of the word "sex" in the constitution to remain male and female instead of being expanded to be "sexual orientation."[122]

Seychelles

An archipelago nation in the Indian Ocean off shore from the African continent, Seychelles historically had been a stopover place for trade between Africa and Asia. The French took control of the Seychelles in 1756 and settlers started to arrive in 1770.[123] The control of the archipelago, together with Mauritius, was transferred to the British in 1810 after the Napoleonic Wars, which was formalized through the Treaty of Paris in 1814.[124]

Seychelles became a separate crown colony in 1903 from Mauritius, and the country achieved independence in 1976 while remaining a member of the British Commonwealth. Seychelles is also member of the African Union.

The population in Seychelles is quite small with only around 95 thousand people, and its GDP per capita was estimated at $15,000 in 2016, which means it is a relatively wealthy country.[125] As a popular tourist destination, the tourism industry accounts for a lion's share of the country's economy. Seychelles did not have an indigenous population before the colonial period, and its demographic composition represents a mixture of colonial settlers, African slaves, and imported laborers from Asia. In terms of religion, the majority are Roman Catholics, which accounts for 76 percent of the total, while Protestants account for another 10 percent.[126]

During the colonial time, Seychelles maintained a penal code that criminalized homosexuality. According to the 1955 version of the law, article 151 listed the following:

> Any person who – a) has carnal knowledge of any person against the order of nature or b) has carnal knowledge of an animal, or c) permits a male person to have carnal knowledge of him or her against the order of nature, is guilty of a felony, and is liable to imprisonment for fourteen years.[127]

Then article 152 stipulated seven years in prison for any attempts to commit the acts mentioned here. The wording is almost exactly the same as the one in Fiji. The law remained the same after independence, although it was claimed that it is rarely enforced.[128] On the other hand, Seychelles' constitution nevertheless confirms individuals' fundamental rights, which include "the rights of the individual to life, liberty and the pursuit of happiness free from all types of discrimination."[129] Thus there existed this contradiction between the constitutional provision of antidiscrimination and the de jure criminalization of homosexuality.

During the 2011 United Nations universal periodic review on Seychelles, the country was given a set of recommendations by a list of European and Latin American countries to get rid of discrimination on sexual orientation and to decriminalize homosexuality.[130] In response to these recommendations, the Seychelles government issued the following statement, "The one provision in the Penal Code for 'sodomy' does not directly discriminate homosexuals as it is intended for penalizing the offence of sodomy as such. In any case this provision has never been applied against anyone." Furthermore, the government promised that it "will decide as to when and to what extent the legislation could be amended to better guarantee the Constitutional precept that lesbian, gay, bisexual and transsexual persons are not to be discriminated in Seychelles."[131]

It took the country another five years to finally decriminalize homosexuality. On May 18, 2016, Seychelles National Assembly passed an amendment to the penal code that got rid of the sodomy criminalization clause. This was done as a result of the pledge made by the President James Michel in his State of the Nation address, during which he stated that there are laws that are no longer relevant, such as "law introduced by the British in 1955 to criminalise homosexuality. Although this law is not enforced these days, it remains part of our legal system. This is an aberration." He then promised that "As a secular and democratic nation, Seychelles has to fulfil its national, international and constitutional obligations. . . . My government has decided to repeal the law. We are submitting a bill to the National Assembly for your consideration."[132] Thus Seychelles joined a list of African countries, such as South Africa, Mozambique, Lesotho, and Sao Tome and Principe, to decriminalize homosexuality in the recent past.[133]

Other than decriminalization of homosexuality, Seychelles also has laws that include protection against discrimination on the basis of sexual orientation. In the 2006 Amendment of the 1995 Employment Act, section 2 defines harassment as "any such unfriendly act, speech or gesture of one person towards another person that is based on the other person's . . . sexual orientation." Additionally, section 46(A) states "Where an employer makes an employment decision against a worker on the grounds of the worker's . . . sexual orientation . . . the worker may make a complaint to the Chief Executive stating all the relevant particulars."[134]

Such progress aside, as a majority Christian country, religious groups in Seychelles did express their dissatisfaction toward the legal change to decriminalize homosexuality when that was announced. For example, the Catholic Church did express that although it respects homosexuals should have dignity it still considers homosexual conduct as morally reprehensible.[135] The Anglican Church also stated that "The church is against the repealing of the law but the church policy is that whether it has been repealed or not, life goes on. We should not discriminate against anyone."[136] At the same time, Seychelles does not have legalized same-sex marriage or civil unions yet. Thus, although social attitudes toward the LGBT community in general are overall relatively tolerant, there is still more that can be done in Seychelles to improve the rights for the LGBT community for more equality.

Conclusion

The six cases reviewed in this chapter have all demonstrated that the success for decriminalization did not come easily but through hard-fought battles either at the legislatures or at the courts. At the same time, the effects of decriminalization of homosexuality have also produced varying degrees of social openness in these societies, and it is in the South African case that the constitutional provision of equality has led to final parity between heterosexual and homosexual persons before law. In all the other five cases, decriminalization aside, anti-decriminalization legislations and/or same-sex partnership legislations have not yet come out in tandem. There are also many LGBT rights organizations and civil society groups whose active mobilizations have played a crucial role in getting rid of this colonial legacy left by the British. Indeed, in the name of rights to human dignity, equality, and privacy, continual criminalization of homosexual conduct has increasingly become difficult to defend, and it is possible that more progressive legislative changes or court rulings will happen in other parts of the world too.

Notes

1 "Hong Kong Profile – Timeline," *BBC News*, July 10, 2017.
2 World Bank Development Indicators.
3 2014 Estimate, CIA World Factbook.
4 "Legal System in Hong Kong," Department of Justice, Hong Kong SAR, accessible at www.doj.gov.hk/eng/legal/.
5 The current ordinance can be accessed at www.elegislation.gov.hk/hk/cap212!en.
6 Records of the repealed articles can be accessed at Historical Laws of Hong Kong Online at http://oelawhk.lib.hku.hk/items/show/2864.
7 Ibid.
8 The Act can be accessed at www.legislation.gov.uk/ukpga/1967/60/pdfs/ukpga_19670060_en.pdf.
9 Carole Petersen, "Values in Transition: The Development of the Gay and Lesbian Rights Movement in Hong Kong," *Loyola of Los Angeles International and Comparative Law Review* 19, no. 2 (January 1, 1997): 340.
10 The report can be accessed at www.hkreform.gov.hk/en/docs/rhomosexualp-e.pdf.
11 Petersen, "Values in Transition," 344.
12 Phil C. W. Chan, "The Lack of Sexual Orientation Anti-Discrimination Legislation in Hong Kong: Breach of International and Domestic Legal Obligations," *The International Journal of Human Rights* 9, no. 1 (March 1, 2005): 71.
13 John Cheo, "Gay and Lesbian Rights in Confucian Asia: The Case of Hong Kong, Singapore, and Taiwan," *CUREJ: College Undergraduate Research Electronic Journal, University of Pennsylvania* (2014), 31.
14 Ibid., 31–2.
15 Petersen, "Values in Transition," 349.
16 Ibid., 337.
17 Jasmine Siu, "Hong Kong Man Mounts Legal Challenge against Laws on Gay Sex, Calling Them Discriminatory and Unconstitutional," *South China Morning Post*, October 11, 2017.
18 Petersen, "Values in Transition," 337.
19 The current Sex Discrimination Ordinance can be accessed at www.elegislation.gov.hk/hk/cap480!en.

20 Chan, "The Lack of Sexual Orientation Anti-Discrimination Legislation in Hong Kong," 90.
21 Nikki Sun, "Hong Kong's Equality Watchdog Presses for Law to Protect Sexual Minorities," *South China Morning Post*, March 9, 2017.
22 Yiu-tung Suen, "Lack of Legal Protection Is Driving Sexual Minorities Out of Hong Kong," *South China Morning Post*, February 27, 2017.
23 Chris Lau, "Landmark Win for Gay Hong Kong Civil Servant Over Husband's Benefits," *South China Morning Post*, April 28, 2017.
24 "Hong Kong Gay Rights: British Lesbian Wins Spousal Visa Case," *BBC News*, September 25, 2017.
25 Gender Research Centre of the Hong Kong Institute of Asia-Pacific Studies of the Chinese University of Hong Kong, "Report on Study on Legislation against Discrimination on the Grounds of Sexual Orientation, Gender Identity and Intersex Status" (Hong Kong Equal Opportunities Commission, 2016), 97.
26 Danny Lee, "Calls for Hong Kong to Better Protect LGBT Rights as City Wins Bid to Host 2022 Gay Games," *South China Morning Post*, October 31, 2017.
27 T. R. H. Davenport and Christopher Saunders, *South Africa: A Modern History* (Hampshire, UK; New York: Palgrave Macmillan, 2000), 43.
28 World Bank Development Indicators.
29 "Census in Brief," Statistics South Africa, 2011.
30 CIA World Factbook.
31 2001 Estimate, CIA World Factbook.
32 Gustavo Gomes da Costa Santos, "Decriminalising Homosexuality in Africa: Lessons from the South African Experience," in *Human Rights, Sexual Orientation and Gender Identity in the Commonwealth Struggles for Decriminalisation and Change*, ed. Corinne Lennox and Matthew Waites (London: Human Rights Consortium, Institute of Commonwealth Studies, School of Advanced Study, University of London, 2013), 326.
33 Ryan Goodman, "Beyond the Enforcement Principle: Sodomy Laws, Social Norms, and Social Panoptics," *California Law Review* 89, no. 3 (2001): 676.
34 Santos, "Decriminalising Homosexuality in Africa: Lessons From the South African Experience," 326.
35 Goodman, "Beyond the Enforcement Principle: Sodomy Laws, Social Norms, and Social Panoptics," 677.
36 Santos, "Decriminalising Homosexuality in Africa: Lessons From the South African Experience," 316.
37 Glen Retief, "Keeping Sodom Out of the Laager: State Repression of Homosexuality in Apartheid South Africa," in *Defiant Desire: Gay and Lesbian Lives in South Africa*, ed. Mark Gevisser and Edwin Cameron (New York; London: Routledge, 1995), 100.
38 Goodman, "Beyond the Enforcement Principle: Sodomy Laws, Social Norms, and Social Panoptics," 679.
39 Santos, "Decriminalising Homosexuality in Africa: Lessons From the South African Experience," 318.
40 Edwin Cameron, "'Unapprehended Felons': Gays and Lesbians and the Law in South Africa," in *Defiant Desire: Gay and Lesbian Lives in South Africa*, ed. Mark Gevisser and Edwin Cameron (New York: London: Routledge, 1995), 92.
41 Mark Gevisser, "A Different Fight for Freedom: A History of South African Lesbian and Gay Organization From the 1950s to the 1990s," in *Defiant Desire: Gay and Lesbian Lives in South Africa*, ed. Mark Gevisser and Edwin Cameron (New York; London: Routledge, 1995), 78.

42 Peter Tatchell, "The Moment the ANC Embraced Gay Rights," in *Sex & Politics in South Africa*, ed. Neville Hoad, Karen Martin, and Graeme Reid (Cape Town: Double Storey Books, 2005).
43 Eric Christiansen, "Ending the Apartheid of the Closet: Sexual Orientation in the South African Constitutional Process," *New York University Journal of International Law and Politics* 32, no. 4 (2000): 1012.
44 Santos, "Decriminalising Homosexuality in Africa: Lessons From the South African Experience," 322.
45 Ibid., 323.
46 Ibid., 324.
47 A. J. G. M. Sanders, "Homosexuality and the Law: A Gay Revolution in South Africa?," *Journal of African Law* 41, no. 1 (1997): 105.
48 "Gay Rights Win in South Africa," *BBC News*, October 9, 1998.
49 Goodman, "Beyond the Enforcement Principle: Sodomy Laws, Social Norms, and Social Panoptics," 643.
50 Santos, "Decriminalising Homosexuality in Africa: Lessons from the South African Experience," 329.
51 Vasu Reddy, "Decriminalisation of Homosexuality in Post-Apartheid South Africa: A Brief Legal Case History Review From Sodomy to Marriage," *Agenda* 20, no. 67 (January 1, 2006): 147.
52 Ibid., 147.
53 Paul Johnson, "Challenging the Heteronormativity of Marriage: The Role of Judicial Interpretation and Authority," *Social & Legal Studies* 20, no. 3 (September 1, 2011): 356.
54 Clare Nullis, "Same-Sex Marriage Law Takes Effect in S. Africa," *Washington Post*, December 1, 2006.
55 Pumza Fihlani, "South Africa's Lesbians Fear 'Corrective Rape,'" *BBC News*, June 30, 2011.
56 James Fletcher, "Born Free, Killed by Hate – The Price of Being Gay in South Africa," *BBC News*, April 7, 2016.
57 Louise Vincent and Simon Howell, "'Unnatural,' 'Un-African' and 'Ungodly': Homophobic Discourse in Democratic South Africa," *Sexualities* 17, no. 4 (June 1, 2014): 472–83.
58 www.cypnet.co.uk/ncyprus/history/british/index.html.
59 Maria Hadjipavlou, "The Cyprus Conflict: Root Causes and Implications for Peacebuilding," *Journal of Peace Research* 44, no. 3 (2007): 352.
60 https://unficyp.unmissions.org/.
61 http://mfa.gov.ct.tr/cyprus-negotiation-process/historical-background/.
62 World Bank Development Indicators.
63 Ishtiaq Hussain, "The Tanzimat: Secular Reforms in the Ottoman Empire: A Brief Look at the Adoption of Secular Laws in the Ottoman Empire With a Particular Focus on the Tanzimat Reforms (1839–1876)," *Faith Matters* (2011), 10.
64 http://enacademic.com/dic.nsf/enwiki/9578657.
65 Modinos v. Cyprus (European Court of Human Rights April 22, 1993).
66 Dudgeon vs. The United Kingdom (European Court of Human Rights October 22, 1981).
67 Modinos v. Cyprus.
68 Ibid.
69 Michael Theodoulou, "On Cyprus, Values Clash with Desire to Join EU," *The Christian Science Monitor*, April 28, 1998.
70 Ibid.

71 "Cyprus Church vs. Sodomy Reform," *Newsplanet*, April 9, 1998.
72 Martin Hellicar, "House Passes Gay Sex Bill," *Cyprus Mail*, May 22, 1998.
73 George Psyllides, "Controversial Age of Consent Bill Is Passed," *Cyprus Mail*, n.d.
74 www.humandignitytrust.org/pages/OUR%20WORK/Cases/Northern%20 Cyprus.
75 Dasha Afanasieva, "Northern Cyprus Becomes Last European Territory to Decriminalize Gay Sex," *Reuters*, January 27, 2014.
76 Owen Bowcott, "Northern Cyprus Votes to Legalise Gay Sex," *The Guardian*, January 27, 2014.
77 Nicos Trimikliniotis and Corina Demetriou, "Evaluating the Anti-Discrimination Law in the Republic of Cyprus: A Critical Reflection," *The Cyprus Review* 22, no. 2 (2008): 102.
78 Human Rights Campaign, "Cyprus Adds Sexual Orientation and Gender Identity to Anti-Discrimination Law," October 10, 2013.
79 Constantinos Psillides, "Cabinet Approves Bill on Civil Partnerships," *Cyprus Mail*, May 6, 2015.
80 "Gay Rights Groups Build Alliances to Counter Climate of Fear," *Between the Lines News*, October 27, 2016.
81 "The Social Situation Concerning Homophobia and Discrimination on Grounds of Sexual Orientation in Cyprus," *Danish Institute of Human Rights* (March 2009), 4.
82 Angelos Anastasiou, "Storm of Protest Over Archbishop's Anti-Gay Comments," *Cyprus Mail*, March 9, 2014.
83 "Our View: Archbishop's Outburst Against Homosexuality Beyond Offensive," *Cyprus Mail*, November 4, 2016.
84 Satish Chand, "The Political Economy of Fiji: Past, Present, and Prospects," *The Round Table* 104, no. 2 (March 4, 2015): 200.
85 Ibid., 203.
86 World Bank Development Indicators.
87 2007 Estimate, CIA World Factbook.
88 Ibid.
89 For record of the full text of the Fijian Penal Code, see www.paclii.org/fj/legis/consol_act_OK/pc66/.
90 Ibid.
91 For record of the full text of the 1997 Fiji Constitution, see www.wipo.int/edocs/lexdocs/laws/en/fj/fj011en.pdf.
92 Brij V. Lal, "Making History, Becoming History: Reflections on Fijian Coups and Constitutions," *Contemporary Pacific; Honolulu* 14, no. 1 (Spring 2002): 166.
93 Nicole George, "Contending Masculinities and the Limits of Tolerance: Sexual Minorities in Fiji," *The Contemporary Pacific* 20, no. 1 (2008): 166.
94 "Fiji: Sodomy Law Convictions Violate Constitution," *Human Rights Watch*, April 12, 2005.
95 Ibid.
96 McCoskar v. The State (Fiji High Court August 26, 2005).
97 Ibid.
98 "Fiji First Pacific Island Nation With Colonial-Era Sodomy Laws to Formally to Decriminalize Homosexuality," *UNAIDS*, March 4, 2010.
99 Authority of the Fiji Government, "Crime Degree 2009" (2009).
100 For records of the Fiji Marriage Act, see www.paclii.org/fj/legis/consol_act_OK/ma85/.

101 Chris D'Angelo, "Fiji Prime Minister Tells Gay Couples to Move to Iceland," *The Huffington Post*, June 1, 2016.
102 "Differences Here Over Australia's Recent Same-Sex Marriage Vote," *Fiji Sun*, November 18, 2017.
103 Joseph Patrick McCormick, "Fiji: LGBT Rights Campaigners Say Discrimination Remains a Major Issue," *Pink News*, May 16, 2013.
104 Tim Merrill, ed., *Belize: A Country Study* (Washington, DC: GPO for the Library of Congress, 1992), n.p.
105 Ibid.
106 World Bank Development Indicators.
107 2010 Estimate, CIA World Factbook.
108 Ibid.
109 For record of the previous penal code, see www.oas.org/juridico/mla/en/blz/en_blz-int-text-cc.pdf.
110 "About Orozco v. AG," Faculty of Law University of West Indies Rights Advocacy Project (U-RAP), accessible at www.u-rap.org/web2/index.php/2015-09-29-00-40-03/orozco-v-attorney-general-of-belize/item/2-caleb-orozco-v-attorney-general-of-belize-and-others.
111 "Belize: Anti-Homosexuality Legal Provision Struck Down for First Time in Caribbean," *Library of Congress Global Legal Monitor*, August 19, 2016.
112 Julia Scott, "The Lonely Fight Against Belize's Antigay Laws," *The New York Times Magazine*, May 22, 2015.
113 For full text of Belize's Constitution, see www.constituteproject.org/constitution/Belize_2011.pdf?lang=en.
114 Caleb Orozco v. The Attorney General of Belize (The Supreme Court of Belize August 10, 2016).
115 Ibid.
116 "LGBT Rights: Important Legal Precedent in the Caribbean," *Erasing 76 Crimes*, June 13, 2016.
117 Marion Ali, "Surveys Reveal Homophobia Is Down; Domestic Abuse, Teenage Sex Are Up," *The Reporters*, April 18, 2015.
118 For full text of Belize's Immigration Act, see www.belizelaw.org/web/lawadmin/PDF%20files/cap156.pdf.
119 Maurice Tomlinson v. The State of Belize and The State of Trinidad & Tobago (Caribbean Court of Justice June 10, 2016).
120 Ibid.
121 "Sodomy Verdict Appeal Gains Ground in Belize," *Belize Prayer Network*, September 14, 2016.
122 "Belize Government Opens Door for Appeal of Court Ruling that Legalized Gay Sex," *Caribbean 360* (September 12, 2016).
123 A brief history of Seychelles can be accessed on the country page at the Commonwealth website at http://thecommonwealth.org/our-member-countries/seychelles/history.
124 Ibid.
125 World Bank Development Indicators.
126 CIA Country.
127 Records of Seychelles' Penal Code can be accessed at www.refworld.org/docid/4d67afc82.html.
128 www.refugeelegalaidinformation.org/seychelles-lgbti-resources.
129 Records of Seychelles' Constitution can be accessed at www.wipo.int/wipolex/en/text.jsp?file_id=230031.

130 For the list of recommendations, see www.upr-info.org/database/index.php?limit=0&f_SUR=152&f_SMR=All&order=&orderDir=ASC&orderP=true&f_Issue=All&searchReco=&resultMax=300&response=&action_type=&session=&SuRRgrp=&SuROrg=&SMRRgrp=&SMROrg=&pledges=RecoOnly.

131 http://madikazemi.blogspot.hk/2011/10/seychelles-to-decriminalise.html.

132 Transcript of the speech can be accessed at www.statehouse.gov.sc/speeches.php?news_id=2995.

133 Saurav Jung Thapa, "Seychelles Decriminalizes Same-Sex Activity," *Human Rights Campaign*, May 18, 2016.

134 Records of the Seychelles 1995 Employment Act can be accessed at www.ilo.org/wcmsp5/groups/public/-ed_protect/-protrav/-ilo_aids/documents/legaldocument/wcms_127612.pdf.

135 "Seychelles Parliament Passes Bill to Decriminalize Sodomy," *Seychelles News Agency*, May 18, 2016.

136 Nshira Turkson, "A Victory for LGBT Rights in Seychelles," *The Atlantic*, May 19, 2016.

6 Conclusion

This book represents a coordinated effort to document the spread by British colonialism of a legacy of criminalization of homosexual conduct and other violations of LGBT rights across the world. Specifically, penal and criminal codes criminalizing homosexuality have been significant both in the presence of such laws and also in the nature of the laws, such as harshness of penalty. Many of the laws imposed by the British or otherwise adopted because of British influence have prolonged criminalization after independence. Legal path dependence thus has proven to be one of the main factors that explain this dark British colonial legacy. As we have seen in some of the case studies in Chapter 4, the lingering effect of these colonial era laws is quite powerful. However, there is no clear evidence that former British colonies have taken longer to decriminalize than other ex-colonies or other countries with such a law.

On the other hand, there is also a discourse among many countries that have such criminalization measures to defend against Western pressure to decriminalize homosexuality. As we briefly commented in the introduction, many such discourses tend to portray homosexuality as a Western import of a corrupted morality, ignoring the prevalent existence of homosexuality before Western colonization. In Africa, for example, many such discourses often portray homosexuality as "unAfrican," and anti-homosexuality mobilizations have taken on a nationalist tone.[1] As our research has demonstrated, it is most likely the opposite. It was British colonialism that brought this aversion to homosexuality to its colonies rather than homosexuality itself. When existing governments resist pressure to decriminalize, they often cite unfavorable public opinion, which totally ignored the historical construction of such homophobia and its colonial origin.

We also notice two broad strands of causality of political and historical changes. Throughout this book, we have documented how with the spread of the British Empire, a set of penal codes that prohibited homosexual conduct were introduced into the vast spread of territories that came under British control. Although these laws were overall similar, there were in fact tremendous variations in terms of how they were drafted and the level of penalization for each colony. As we have seen in Chapter 2, there was almost no centralized coordination in the introduction of these laws. In some episodes, like the drafting and application in East Africa of the model criminal code for the colonies in the 1920s, or the separate attempted codification of a model code for British territories in the Persian Gulf in the 1950s, there was some explicit effort at coordination. However, the majority of the processes of the spread of criminalization covered in Chapter 2 were not centrally coordinated. Instead, a variety of relatively idiosyncratic factors, including in several cases the fact that a colonial administrator happened to have dealt with the introduction of a criminal code in their previous posting, seem to have been relevant to why a particular criminal code was introduced into a territory, or why one was introduced at all.

On the other hand, we do notice that the decriminalization of homosexuality came through as a result of active political mobilization and hard-won legal battles, such as in the case of Belize. In some other instances they came through as tangential outcomes of broader political processes. For example, in the Hong Kong case as we discussed in Chapter 5, the decriminalization came through a broader political push for more human rights protection in the territory facing imminent return to Chinese sovereignty, rather than through a targeted political campaign. Similarly, in many other countries, decriminalization came through as a result of democratization and/or an introduction of a more progressive constitution, which made continual criminalization difficult to defend on issues of privacy, dignity, and equality. Therefore, we have to take note of such tangential causal mechanisms of political change.

Thus, for the remaining 70 plus countries that continue to criminalize homosexuality, what are the things that can be done to reform their penal codes that can respect and protect the dignity, privacy, and equality of the LGBT community? Obviously, the international LGBT community and human rights groups need to put high pressure on these countries, especially the ones that are actively persecuting sexual minorities. These countries need to be ashamed for their discriminatory and unjust treatment of their citizens on the basis of sexual orientation. The international community needs to put more emphasis on the fact that gay rights are human rights, and thus need to have a concerted effort to combat continual criminalization of homosexuality. Furthermore, there is more need for the international media to focus on how British colonialism spread homophobia rather than the counter-discourse of how the West exported homosexuality to the rest of the world.

On the other hand, from the experiences of some of the recent successful cases, we can see that judicial litigation is one fruitful way where constitutional provisions of equality and privacy, which might exist in many countries' constitutions, can be effectively utilized to force such legal changes. International LGBT organizations and human rights groups should utilize their resources to support many such legal battles around the world.

Note

1 Neville Hoad, *African Intimacies: Race, Homosexuality, and Globalization* (Minneapolis: University of Minnesota Press, 2007); Marc Epprecht, *Heterosexual Africa?: The History of an Idea From the Age of Exploration to the Age of AIDS* (Athens; Scottsville, South Africa: Ohio University Press, 2008).

Bibliography

Abrams, Norman. "Interpreting the Criminal Code Ordinance, 1935 – The Untapped Well." *Israel Law Review* 7, no. 1 (1972).

Alam, M. S. "Colonialism, Decolonisation and Growth Rates: Theory and Empirical Evidence." *Cambridge Journal of Economics* 18, no. 3 (June 1, 1994): 235–58.

Alesina, Alberto, Arnaud Devleeschauwer, William Easterly, Sergio Kurlat, and Romain Wacziarg. "Fractionalization." *Journal of Economic Growth* 8, no. 2 (2003): 155–94.

Andersen, Robert, and Tina Fetner. "Economic Inequality and Intolerance: Attitudes Toward Homosexuality in 35 Democracies." *American Journal of Political Science* 52, no. 4 (2008): 942–58.

Anheier, Helmut K., Mary Kaldor, and Marlies Glasius, eds. *Global Civil Society 2006/7*. London: SAGE Publications Ltd, 2006.

Asal, Victor, and Udi Sommer. *Legal Path Dependence and the Long Arm of the Religious State: Sodomy Provisions and Gay Rights Across Nations and Over Time*. Albany, NY: State University of New York Press, 2006.

Asal, Victor, Udi Sommer, and Paul G. Harwood. "Original Sin: A Cross-National Study of the Legality of Homosexual Acts." *Comparative Political Studies* 46, no. 3 (2013): 320–51.

Authority of the Fiji Government. Crime Decree 2009 (2009). www.ilo.org/dyn/natlex/natlex4.detail?p_lang=en&p_isn=86223&p_country=FJI&p_count=296

Bailyn, Bernard, and Philip D. Morgan. *Strangers Within the Realm: Cultural Margins of the First British Empire*. Chapel Hill: UNC Press Books, 2012.

Basnayake, Sinha. "The Anglo-Indian Codes in Ceylon." *International and Comparative Law Quarterly* 22, no. 2 (1973): 284–311.

Baudh, Sumit. "Decriminalisation of Consensual Same-Sex Sexual Acts in the South Asian Commonwealth: Struggles in Contexts." In *Human Rights, Sexual Orientation and Gender Identity in the Commonwealth: Struggles for Decriminalisation and Change*, 287–311. London: Institute of Commonwealth Studies, School of Advanced Study, University of London, 2013.

"Belize: Anti-Homosexuality Legal Provision Struck Down for First Time in Caribbean." *Library of Congress Global Legal Monitor*, August 19, 2016.

Bernhard, Michael, Christopher Reenock, and Timothy Nordstrom. "The Legacy of Western Overseas Colonialism on Democratic Survival." *International Studies Quarterly* 48, no. 1 (2004): 225–50.

Bijl, Nick van der. *The Mau Mau Rebellion: The Emergency in Kenya 1952–1956*. Barnsley, South Yorkshire: Pen & Sword Military, 2017.
Bohlander, Michael. "Criminalising LGBT Persons Under National Criminal Law and Article 7(1)(h) and (3) of the ICC Statute." *Global Policy* 5, no. 4 (2014): 401–14.
Brewer, I. G. "Sources of the Criminal Law of Botswana." *Journal of African Law* 18, no. 1 (1974).
Brown, Desmond H., ed. *The Birth of a Criminal Code: The Evolution of Canada's Justice System*. Toronto: University of Toronto Press, 1995.
Brown, Kenneth. "Criminal Law and Custom in Solomon Islands." *Queensland University of Technology Law Journal* 2 (1986).
Brown, Nathan J. *The Rule of Law in the Arab World: Courts in Egypt and the Gulf*. Cambridge; New York: Cambridge University Press, 1997.
Bruce-Jones, Eddie, and Lucas Paoli Itaborahy. "State-Sponsored Homophobia: A World Survey of Laws Criminalising Same-Sex Sexual Acts Between Consenting Adults." *ILGA*, 2011.
Bull, Melissa, Susan Pinto, and Paul Wilson. *Homosexual Law Reform in Australia*. Canberra: Australian Institute of Criminology, 1991.
Burack, Cynthia. *Sin, Sex, and Democracy: Antigay Rhetoric and the Christian Right*. Albany, NY: State University of New York Press, 2008.
Caleb Orozco v. The Attorney General of Belize (The Supreme Court of Belize August 10, 2016).
Cameron, Edwin. "'Unapprehended Felons': Gays and Lesbians and the Law in South Africa." In *Defiant Desire: Gay and Lesbian Lives in South Africa*, edited by Mark Gevisser and Edwin Cameron. New York; London: Routledge, 1995.
Carroll, Aengus, and Lucas Ramon Mendos. "State-Sponsored Homophobia: A World Survey of Sexual Orientation Laws." *ILGA*, 2017.
Chan, Phil C. W. "The Lack of Sexual Orientation Anti-Discrimination Legislation in Hong Kong: Breach of International and Domestic Legal Obligations." *The International Journal of Human Rights* 9, no. 1 (March 1, 2005): 69–106.
Chand, Satish. "The Political Economy of Fiji: Past, Present, and Prospects." *The Round Table* 104, no. 2 (March 4, 2015): 199–208.
Cheo, John. "Gay and Lesbian Rights in Confucian Asia: The Case of Hong Kong, Singapore, and Taiwan." *CUREJ: College Undergraduate Research Electronic Journal, University of Pennsylvania*, 2014.
Chernilo, Daniel. "Social Theory's Methodological Nationalism: Myth and Reality." *European Journal of Social Theory* 9, no. 1 (February 1, 2006): 5–22.
Christiansen, Eric. "Ending the Apartheid of the Closet: Sexual Orientation in the South African Constitutional Process." *New York University Journal of International Law and Politics* 32, no. 4 (2000): 997–1058.
Chua Kher Shing, Lynette J. "Saying No: Sections 377 and 377A of the Penal Code." *Singapore Journal of Legal Studies* (2003): 209–61.
"Criminalization of Homosexuality: Guyana." *Human Dignity Trust*, October 25, 2015.
Crompton, Louis. *Homosexuality and Civilization*. Cambridge, MA: Harvard University Press, 2003.

Darr, Orna Alyagon. "Narratives of 'Sodomy' and 'Unnatural Offenses' in the Courts of Mandate Palestine (1918–48)." *Law and History Review* 35, no. 1 (2017): 235–60. https://doi.org/10.1017/S0738248016000493.

Davenport, T. R. H., and Christopher Saunders. *South Africa: A Modern History*. Hampshire; New York: Palgrave Macmillan, 2000.

Department of Sociology, Psychology and Social Work, University of West Indies, Mona. "National Survey of Attitudes and Perceptions of Jamaicans Towards Same Sex Relationships." *J-FLAG; AIDS-Free World*, 2012.

De Young, James B. *Homosexuality: Contemporary Claims Examined in Light of the Bible and Other Ancient Literature and Law*. Grand Rapids, MI: Kregel Academic & Professional, 2000."Documentation of Country Conditions Regarding the Treatment of Gay Men, Lesbians, Bisexuals, and Transgender Individuals in Guyana." *Columbia Law School Sexuality and Gender Law Clinic*, May 2017.

Dudgeon v. The United Kingdom (European Court of Human Rights October 22, 1981).

Epprecht, Marc. *Heterosexual Africa?: The History of an Idea From the Age of Exploration to the Age of AIDS*. Athens; Scottsville, South Africa: Ohio University Press, 2008.

Ferguson, Niall. *Empire: The Rise and Demise of the British World Order and the Lessons for Global Power*. New York: Basic Books, 2003.

Finerty, Courtney E. "Being Gay in Kenya: The Implications of Kenya's New Constitution for Its Anti-Sodomy Laws." *Cornell International Law Journal* (2012): 431–59.

Frank, David John, Steven A. Boutcher, and Bayliss Camp. "The Reform of Sodomy Laws: From a World Society Perspective." In *Queer Mobilizations: LGBT Activists Confront the Law*, edited by S. Barclay, M. Berstein, and A. M. Marshall. New York: New York University Press, 2009.

Frank, David John, Bayliss Camp, and Steven A. Boutcher. "Worldwide Trends in the Criminal Regulation of Sex, 1945 to 2005." *American Sociological Review* 75, no. 6 (2010): 867–93.

Friedland, Martin L. "Codification in the Commonwealth: Earlier Efforts." *Commonwealth Law Bulletin* 18, no. 3 (1992): 1172–80.

———. "R. S. Wright's Model Criminal Code: A Forgotten Chapter in the History of the Criminal Law." *Oxford Journal of Legal Studies* 1, no. 3 (1981): 307–46.

Gardner, William James. *The History of Jamaica: From Its Discovery by Christopher Columbus to the Year 1872*. New York: Routledge, 2005.

Gaskins Jr., Joseph. "'Buggery' and the Commonwealth Caribbean: A Comparative Examination of the Bahamas, Jamaica, and Trinidad and Tobago." In *Human Rights, Sexual Orientation and Gender Identity in the Commonwealth: Struggles for Decriminalisation and Change*, 429–54. London: Institute of Commonwealth Studies, School of Advanced Study, University of London, 2013.

Gender Research Centre of the Hong Kong Institute of Asia-Pacific Studies of the Chinese University of Hong Kong. "Report on Study on Legislation Against Discrimination on the Grounds of Sexual Orientation, Gender Identity and Intersex Status." *Hong Kong Equal Opportunities Commission*, 2016.

George, Nicole. "Contending Masculinities and the Limits of Tolerance: Sexual Minorities in Fiji." *The Contemporary Pacific* 20, no. 1 (2008): 163–89.

Gevisser, Mark. "A Different Fight for Freedom: A History of South African Lesbian and Gay Organization From the 1950s to the 1990s." In *Defiant Desire: Gay and Lesbian Lives in South Africa*, edited by Mark Gevisser and Edwin Cameron. New York; London: Routledge, 1995.

Gibbs, Harry. "Queensland Criminal Code: From Italy to Zanzibar." *Australian Law Journal* 77, no. 4 (2003): 232–9.

"The Global Divide on Homosexuality." *Pew Research Center*, 2013.

Goodman, Ryan. "Beyond the Enforcement Principle: Sodomy Laws, Social Norms, and Social Panoptics." *California Law Review* 89, no. 3 (2001): 643–740.

Gupta, Alok. "Section 377 and the Dignity of Indian Homosexuals." *Economic and Political Weekly*, November 18, 2006.

———. *This Alien Legacy: The Origins of "Sodomy" Laws in British Colonialism*. New York: Human Rights Watch, 2008.

"Guyana 2014 Human Rights Report." *Country Reports on Human Rights 2014*. United States Department of State, 2014.

Hadjipavlou, Maria. "The Cyprus Conflict: Root Causes and Implications for Peacebuilding." *Journal of Peace Research* 44, no. 3 (2007): 349–65.

Han, Enze, and Joseph O'Mahoney. "British Colonialism and the Criminalization of Homosexuality." *Cambridge Review of International Affairs* 27, no. 2 (2014): 268–88.

Hoad, Neville. *African Intimacies: Race, Homosexuality, and Globalization*. Minneapolis: University of Minnesota Press, 2007.

Hor, Michael. "Enforcement of 377A: Entering the Twilight Zone." In *Queer Singapore: Illiberal Citizenship and Mediated Cultures*, edited by Audrey Yue and Jun Zubillaga-Pow. Hong Kong: Hong Kong University Press, 2012.

"Human Rights Violations Against Lesbian, Gay, Bisexual, and Transgender (LGBT) People in Jamaica: A Shadow Report." *J-FLAG; Women's Empowerment for Change (WE-Change); The Colour Pink Foundation; TransWave; Center for International Human Rights, Northwestern Pritzker School of Law of Northwestern University; Global Initiatives for Human Rights of Heartland Alliance for Human Needs & Human Rights*, October 2016.

Huntington, Samuel P. "Will More Countries Become Democratic?" *Political Science Quarterly* 99, no. 2 (1984): 193–218.

Hussain, Ishtiaq. "The Tanzimat: Secular Reforms in the Ottoman Empire: A Brief Look at the Adoption of Secular Laws in the Ottoman Empire With a Particular Focus on the Tanzimat Reforms (1839–1876)." *Faith Matters*, 2011.

Inglehart, Ronald. *Culture Shift in Advanced Industrial Society*. Princeton, NJ: Princeton University Press, 1990.

Inglehart, Ronald, and Christian Welzel. *Modernization, Cultural Change, and Democracy: The Human Development Sequence*. Cambridge: Cambridge University Press, 2005.

Jackman, Mahalia. "Protecting the Fabric of Society? Heterosexual Views on the Usefulness of the Anti-Gay Laws in Barbados, Guyana and Trinidad and Tobago." *Culture, Health & Sexuality* 19, no. 1 (January 2, 2017): 91–106.

Jjuuko, Adrian. "The Incremental Approach: Uganda's Struggle for the Decriminalisation of Homosexuality." In *The Commonwealth: Struggles for Decriminalisation and Change*, London: Institute of Commonwealth Studies, School of Advanced Study, University of London, 381–408, 2013.

Kadish, Sanford H. "Codifiers of the Criminal Law: Wechsler's Predecessors." *Columbia Law Review* 78, no. 5 (1978): 1098–1144.

Kang, Wenqing. *Obsession: Male Same-Sex Relations in China, 1900–1950*. Queer Asia. Hong Kong; London: Hong Kong University Press, 2009.

Kenya Human Rights Commission. "The Outlawed Amongst US: A Study of the LGBTI Community's Search for Equality and Non-Discrimination in Kenya." *Nairobi, Kenya*, 2011.

Kerr, A. J. "The Reception and Codification of Systems of Law in Southern Africa." *Journal of African Law* 2, no. 2 (1958): 82–100.

Kham, Nang Yin. "An Introduction to the Law and Judicial System of Myanmar." *CALS Working Paper Series 14/2*, March 2014.

Kirby, Michael. "Discrimination on the Ground of Sexual Orientation: A New Initiative for the Commonwealth of Nations?" *The Commonwealth Lawyer*, May 2007.

Klerman, Daniel M., Paul G. Mahoney, Holger Spamann, and Mark I. Weinstein. "Legal Origin or Colonial History?" *Journal of Legal Analysis* 3, no. 2 (December 1, 2011): 379–409.

Kolsky, Elizabeth. "Codification and the Rule of Colonial Difference: Criminal Procedure in British India." *Law and History Review* 23, no. 3 (2005): 631–83.

Köndgen, Olaf. *The Codification of Islamic Criminal Law in the Sudan: Penal Codes and Supreme Court Case Law under Numayrī and Al-Bashīr*. Leiden: Brill, 2017.

Lal, Brij V. "Making History, Becoming History: Reflections on Fijian Coups and Constitutions." *Contemporary Pacific; Honolulu* 14, no. 1 (Spring 2002): 148.

Landes, David S. *The Wealth and Poverty of Nations: Why Some Are So Rich and Some So Poor*. New York: W. W. Norton & Company, 1999.

Lange, Matthew. *Lineages of Despotism and Development: British Colonialism and State Power*. Chicago: University of Chicago Press, 2009.

Lange, Matthew, James Mahoney, and Matthias vom Hau. "Colonialism and Development: A Comparative Analysis of Spanish and British Colonies." *American Journal of Sociology* 111, no. 5 (2006): 1412–62.

La Porta, Rafael, Florencio López-de-Silanes, Cristian Pop-Eleches, and Andrei Shleifer. "Judicial Checks and Balances." *Journal of Political Economy* 112, no. 2 (2004): 445–70.

La Porta, Rafael, Florencio Lopez-de-Silanes, Andrei Shleifer, and Robert Vishny. "The Quality of Government." *Journal of Law, Economics and Organization* 15, no. 1 (1999): 222–79.

Leggett, Ian. *Uganda*. Oxford: Oxfam, 2001.

LePoer, Barbara Leitch. *Singapore: A Country Study*. Washington, DC: Library of Congress, 1991. https://archive.org/details/singaporecountry00lepo.

Leslie, Christopher R. "Creating Criminals: The Injuries Inflicted by Unenforced Sodomy Laws." *Harvard Civil Rights-Civil Liberties Law Review* 35, no. 1 (2000): 103–82.

Liebesny, Herbert J. "Administration and Legal Development in Arabia: The Persian Gulf Principalities." *Middle East Journal* 10, no. 1 (1956): 33–42.

Lipset, Seymour Martin. *A Comparative Analysis of the Social Requisites of Democracy*. Oxford: Blackwell Publishers, 2004.

Long, Scott. "Before the Law: Criminalizing Sexual Conduct in Colonial and Post-colonial Southern African Societies." In *More than a Name: State-Sponsored Homophobia and Its Consequences in Southern Africa*, edited by Human Rights Watch & The International Gay and Lesbian Human Rights Commission. New York: Human Rights Watch, 2009.

Louise Vincent, and Simon Howell. " 'Unnatural,' 'Un-African' and 'Ungodly': Homophobic Discourse in Democratic South Africa." *Sexualities* 17, no. 4 (June 1, 2014): 472–83.

"Love, Hate and the Law: Decriminalizing Homosexuality." London: Amnesty International, 2008.

Macaulay, Thomas Babington Baron Macaulay. *The Indian Penal Code, as Originally Framed in 1837*. Madras: Higginbotham, 1888.

Mackenzie, Geraldine. "An Enduring Influence: Sir Samuel Griffith and His Contribution to Criminal Justice in Queensland." *Queensland University of Technology Law & Justice Journal* 2, no. 1 (2002).

Mahoney, James. "Path Dependence in Historical Sociology." *Theory and Society* 29, no. 4 (2000): 507–48.

Malupande, Sydney. "Human Rights in Zambia: Freedom of Sexual Orientation, Homosexual Law Reform." LLB Thesis, University of Zambia, 2000.

Maurice Tomlinson v. The State of Belize and The State of Trinidad & Tobago (Caribbean Court of Justice June 10, 2016).

McClain, William. "Criminal Law Treatment of Sexual Activity." *University of Lesotho Faculty of Social Sciences Staff Seminar Paper No. 19*, 1979.

McCoskar v The State (Fiji High Court August 26, 2005).

Merrill, Tim, ed. *Belize: A Country Study*. Washington, DC: GPO for the Library of Congress, 1992.

———, ed. *Guyana and Belize: Country Studies*. Washington, DC: Library of Congress, 1992.

Metcalf, Barbara D., and Thomas R. Metcalf. *A Concise History of Modern India*. 3rd edition. Cambridge, UK; New York: Cambridge University Press, 2012.

Miles, William F. S. *Hausaland Divided: Colonialism and Independence in Nigeria and Niger*. Ithaca: Cornell University Press, 1994.

Misra, Geetanjali. "Decriminalising Homosexuality in India." *Reproductive Health Matters* 17, no. 34 (November 1, 2009): 20–8.

Modinos v. Cyprus (European Court of Human Rights April 22, 1993).

Morris, Henry Francis. "A History of the Adoption of Codes of Criminal Law and Procedure in British Colonial Africa, 1876–1935." *Journal of African Law* 18, no. 1 (1974): 6–23.

———. "How Nigeria Got Its Criminal Code." *Journal of African Law* 14, no. 3 (1970): 137–54.

Morris, Henry Francis, and James S. Read. *Indirect Rule and the Search for Justice: Essays in East African Legal History*. Oxford: Oxford University Press, 1972.

Murray, Stephen O. *Homosexualities*. Worlds of Desire. Chicago: University of Chicago Press, 2000.

Murray, Stephen O., and Will Roscoe, eds. *Boy-Wives and Female Husbands: Studies in African Homosexualities*. New York: Palgrave, 1998.

Mutibwa, Phares Mukasa. *Uganda Since Independence: A Story of Unfulfilled Hopes*. London: C. Hurst & Co. Publishers, 1992.

Norris, Pippa, and Ronald Inglehart. *Cosmopolitan Communications: Cultural Diversity in a Globalized World*. New York: Cambridge University Press, 2009.

"Not Safe at Home: Violence and Discrimination Against LGBT People in Jamaica." *Human Rights Watch*, October 21, 2014.

Olsson, Ola. "On the Democratic Legacy of Colonialism." *Journal of Comparative Economics* 37, no. 4 (2009): 534–51.

O'Regan, Robin S. *New Essays on the Australian Criminal Codes*. Sydney: Law Book Company, 1988.

———. "Sir Samuel Griffith's Criminal Code." *Journal of the Royal Historical Society of Queensland* 14, no. 8 (1991): 305–17.

Paul Johnson. "Challenging the Heteronormativity of Marriage: The Role of Judicial Interpretation and Authority." *Social & Legal Studies* 20, no. 3 (September 1, 2011): 349–67.

Petersen, Carole. "Values in Transition: The Development of the Gay and Lesbian Rights Movement in Hong Kong." *Loyola of Los Angeles International and Comparative Law Review* 19, no. 2 (January 1, 1997): 337.

Pochhammer, Wilhelm Von. *India's Road to Nationhood: A Political History of the Subcontinent*. New Delhi: Allied Publishers, 1992.

Radics, George Baylon. "Decolonizing Singapore's Sex Laws: Tracing Section 377A of Singapore's Penal Code." *Columbia Human Rights Law Review* 45, no. 1 (2013): 57–99.

Read, James S. "Ghana: The Criminal Code, 1960." *International and Comparative Law Quarterly* 11, no. 1 (1962): 272–9.

Reddy, Vasu. "Decriminalisation of Homosexuality in Post-Apartheid South Africa: A Brief Legal Case History Review From Sodomy to Marriage." *Agenda* 20, no. 67 (January 1, 2006): 146–57.

Regan, Tristan. "Uganda's Anti Homosexuality Act 2014: A Perspective on the Developmental Consequences." Master Thesis, Aalborg University, 2014.

Retief, Glen. "Keeping Sodom Out of the Laager: State Repression of Homosexuality in Apartheid South Africa." In *Defiant Desire: Gay and Lesbian Lives in South Africa*, edited by Mark Gevisser and Edwin Cameron. New York; London: Routledge, 1995.

Sanders, A. J. G. M. "Homosexuality and the Law: A Gay Revolution in South Africa?" *Journal of African Law* 41, no. 1 (1997): 100–8.

Sanders, Douglas E. "377 and the Unnatural Afterlife of British Colonialism in Asia." *Asian Journal of Comparative Law* 4 (2009): 1–49. https://doi.org/10.1017/S2194607800000417.

Santos, Gustavo Gomes da Costa. "Decriminalising Homosexuality in Africa: Lessons From the South African Experience." In *Human Rights, Sexual Orientation and Gender Identity in the Commonwealth Struggles for Decriminalisation and Change*, edited by Corinne Lennox and Matthew Waites. London: Human Rights Consortium, Institute of Commonwealth Studies, School of Advanced Study, University of London, 2013.

Schmitt, Arno, and Jehoeda Sofer. *Sexuality and Eroticism Among Males in Moslem Societies*. Binghamton, NY: Routledge, 1992.

Sibalis, Michael David. "Regulation of Male Homosexuality in Revolutionary and Napoleonic France, 1789–1815." In *Homosexuality in Modern France*, edited by Jeffrey Merrick and Bryant T. Ragan. New York: Oxford University Press, 1996.

Singh, Ravin. "President to Respect LGBT Rights." *Guyana Chronicle*, January 6, 2016.

Skuy, David. "Macaulay and the Indian Penal Code of 1862: The Myth of the Inherent Superiority and Modernity of the English Legal System Compared to India's Legal System in the Nineteenth Century." *Modern Asian Studies* 32 (1998): 513–57.

Smith, Delores E. "Homophobic and Transphobic Violence Against Youth: The Jamaican Context." *International Journal of Adolescence and Youth* (June 15, 2017): 1–9.

"The Social Situation Concerning Homophobia and Discrimination on Grounds of Sexual Orientation in Cyprus." *Danish Institute of Human Rights*, March 2009.

Society Against Sexual Orientation Discrimination (SASOD) Guyana. "On Devil's Island: A UPR Submission on LGBT Human Rights in Guyana." *Sexual Rights Initiative*, 2014.

———. "Stakeholder Report to the UN Committee on Economic, Social and Cultural Rights on the Protection of the Rights of LGBTI Persons in Guyana." *Society Against Sexual Orientation Discrimination (SASOD)*, August 2015.

"Speaking Out: The Rights of LGBTI Citizens From Across the Commonwealth." *Kaleidoscope Trust*, 2013.

Suood, Husnu Al. *The Maldivian Legal System*. Male: Maldives Law Institute, 2014.

Tatchell, Peter. "The Moment the ANC Embraced Gay Rights." In *Sex & Politics in South Africa*, edited by Neville Hoad, Karen Martin, and Graeme Reid. Cape Town: Double Storey Books, 2005.

Teng, Laurence Leong Wai. "Decoding Sexual Policy in Singapore." In *Social Policy in Post-Industrial Singapore*, edited by Lian Kwen Fee and Tong Chee Kiong. Leiden; Boston: Brill, 2008.

Tielman, Robert, and Hans Hammelburg. "World Survey on the Social and Legal Position of Gays and Lesbians." In *The Third Pink Book: A Global View of Lesbian and Gay Liberation and Oppression*, edited by Aart Hendriks, Robert Tielman, and Evert van der Veen. Buffalo, NY: Prometheus Books, 1993.

Trimikliniotis, Nicos, and Corina Demetriou. "Evaluating the Anti-Discrimination Law in the Republic of Cyprus: A Critical Reflection." *The Cyprus Review* 22, no. 2 (2008).

Vanita, Ruth. "Homosexuality in India: Past and Present." *IIAS Newsletter*, November 1, 2002, 10–11.

———. *Queering India: Same-Sex Love and Eroticism in Indian Culture and Society*. New York: Psychology Press, 2002.

Vanita, Ruth, and Saleem Kidwai, eds. *Same-Sex Love in India: Readings From Literature and History*. Palgrave Macmillan, 2001.

Verghese, Ajay. *The Colonial Origins of Ethnic Violence in India*. Stanford, CA: Stanford University Press, 2016.

Waaldijk, Kees. *Legal Recognition of Homosexual Orientation in the Countries of the World*. Leiden, the Netherlands: Leiden Law School, 2009.

West, Keon, and Noel M. Cowell. "Predictors of Prejudice Against Lesbians and Gay Men in Jamaica." *The Journal of Sex Research* 52, no. 3 (March 24, 2015): 296–305.

Whitecross, Richard W. "The Thrimzhung Chenmo and the Emergence of the Contemporary Bhutanese Legal System." In *The Spider and the Piglet: Collected Papers on Bhutanese Society*, edited by Karma Ura and Sonam Kinga. Thimphu: Center for Bhutan Studies, 2004.

Wilets, Jim. "Divergence Between LGBTI Legal, Political, and Social Progress in the Caribbean and Latin America." In *The Politics of Sexuality in Latin America: A Reader on Lesbian, Gay, Bisexual, and Transgender Rights*, edited by Javier Corrales and Mario Pecheny. Pittsburgh, PA: University of Pittsburgh Press, 2010.

Wright, Barry. "Criminal Law Codification and Imperial Projects: The Self-Governing Jurisdiction Codes of the 1890's." *Legal History* 12, no. 1 (2008): 19–49.

———. "Self-Governing Codifications of English Criminal Law and Empire: The Queensland and Canadian Examples." *University of Queensland Law Journal* 26, no. 1 (2007): 39–65.

Wright, Robert S. *Drafts of a Criminal Code and a Code of Criminal Procedure for the Island of Jamaica With an Explanatory Memorandum*. London: Great Britain Parliament, 1877.

Young, Crawford. *The African Colonial State in Comparative Perspective*. New Haven, CT: Yale University Press, 1997.

Index